The Excellent Education System
Using Six Sigma to Transform Schools

Other books by Daniel T. Bloom

Achieving HR Excellence through Six Sigma

Field Guide to Achieving HR Excellence through Six Sigma

Just Get Me There: A Journey through Corporate Relocation

Advance Praise

"I could not put it down! This is an excellent resource and compelling read for anyone committed to improving their organization's performance. Congratulations, I can't wait to share the book with my colleagues and staff."

—Dr. Bryan Albrecht
President & CEO, Gateway Technical College

"Excellent, excellent, excellent read. Congratulations, this is an amazing book."

—Kamaljit K. Jackson
Quality Systems Manager, Gateway Technical College

"I taught college for many years and wished we would have had this book. Our quests for excellence would have been much more structured, laser focused and successful. Like most educators, we were not versed in the Six Sigma approach and would have greatly benefited from Daniel Bloom's discussion of excellence, comprehensive review of Six Sigma and practical application for the classroom. A hidden benefit would have been how it can provide a framework for communicating between teachers, administration, students, parents, and the taxpayers.

In the end, this book will help schools prepare students by reexamining the process of education, eliminating waste and building a much needed foundation of excellence. It is then that students will thrive in an ever-changing world. I highly recommend it for teachers and administrators ranging from K-12 on through college. If I were scheduling a faculty in-service, this book would be the first place I would start."

—Loren Murfield, PhD

"For the past 20 years I have been applying a combination of Lean, Six Sigma and Theory of Constraints to drive improvement in a variety of fields including manufacturing, healthcare, and maintenance, repair and overhaul. In each case, the results achieved have been outstanding in terms of profitability and flow. I've often wondered how this same approach would work in an academic environment. The good news is, my days of wondering are over, thanks to Dan Bloom!

Dan's new book, *The Excellent Education System: Using Six Sigma to Transform School,* provides educators, at all levels, with the framework and plan for improvement. To quote Dan from his wonderful new book, 'The bottom line is that the TOC segment of the TLS orientation provides answers to three vital questions:

1. TOC tells us what has to be changed
2. TOC tells us what we need to change the process to
3. TOC tells us how to make the change happen

The perspective then moves to the use of Lean tools to remove the obstacles and then the Six Sigma tools to create a standard of work going forward.

Although Dan provides the key attributes for a successful educational improvement initiative, it is these three questions that every educational institution must answer correctly in order to successfully drive their improvement effort.

Dan brilliantly lays out the necessary tools from each improvement methodology and provides relevant examples on how to use them. Dan also tells us that improvement can't just be from the top down. Improvement must come at all levels with active participation at all levels of the organization.

Well done Dan and I highly recommend this book to all administrators, teachers and students!"

—Bob Sproull
Certified LSS MBB and TOC Jonah

"I salute Dan Bloom for asking the right questions and presenting a proven strategy for creating a culture of transformation that is aimed squarely at creating excellence in our educational system. Dan aims his expertise at teacher and student thinking systems in a way that is refreshing, effective, and on point. This book is a must for teachers and administrators looking to create change in the education system."

—Carl Nielson
Chief Discovery Officer, Success Discoveries
Author/Developer, Career Coaching for Students

The Excellent Education System
Using Six Sigma to Transform Schools

Daniel T. Bloom SPHR, SSBB, SCRP

Routledge
Taylor & Francis Group

A PRODUCTIVITY PRESS BOOK

CRC Press
Taylor & Francis Group
6000 Broken Sound Parkway NW, Suite 300
Boca Raton, FL 33487-2742

CRC Press is an imprint of Taylor & Francis Group, an Informa business

No claim to original U.S. Government works

Printed on acid-free paper

International Standard Book Number-13: 978-1-4987-5850-5 (Paperback)
International Standard Book Number-13: 978-1-138-56263-9 (Hardback)
International Standard Book Number-13: 978-1-4987-5851-2 (eBook)

Visit the Taylor & Francis Web site at
http://www.taylorandfrancis.com

and the CRC Press Web site at
http://www.crcpress.com

Contents

List of Acronyms

ASQ	American Society for Quality
CAP	Change Acceleration Process
CEO	Chief Executive Officer
CPA	Certified Public Accountant
DMADV	Define-Measure-Analyze-Design-Verify
DMAIC	Define-Measure-Analyze-Improve-Control
DSS	Design for Six Sigma
FTE	Full-Time Equivalent Employee
GE	General Electric
HR	Human Resources
IT	Information Technology
ITT	International Telephone and Telegraph
KPI	Key Performance Indicator
NLRB	National Labor Relations Board
PDCA	Plan-Do-Check-Act
SIPOC	Suppliers-Inputs-Processes-Outputs-Customers
TLS	Theory of Constraints–Lean–Six Sigma
TOC	Theory of Constraints
TPS	Toyota Production System
TQM	Total Quality Management
VOC	Voice of the Customer
WIFM	What's In It For Me

List of Illustrations

Acknowledgments

Over a decade ago, I began a journey. It was not a journey of self-discovery. It was not a journey to some specific place or time. It was a journey into the reasons why some of our processes were not as smooth running as we would like. It was a journey to explore the inner workings of educational organizations and to gain a more comprehensive perspective on why we do things the way we do. Many of the processes we utilize on an everyday basis, when carefully screened, are hurting us in the long run.

Former First Lady and former Secretary of State Hillary Clinton stated in her book *It Takes a Village* that it takes the efforts of the whole global community to reach the goals we have set for ourselves. Writing a book takes no less of a community to produce the finished product.

When I began the research for this book I was told that no one would be interested. I found just the opposite. I am deeply appreciative of those continuous process improvement and educational professionals who have helped me along the way. If I have left anyone out, I have done so with regret, but I want to thank you.

My effort originally was to determine examples of educational systems across the full breadth of education, but with the exception of Gateway Technical College I found myself centered on the public K–12 schools. While there is not a wide presence in this area, the ones that I did find were of great help. The individuals who were of most assistance to my research were Dr. Bryan Albrecht and Kamaljit Jackson of Gateway Technical College, who willingly provided me with the information regarding the new normal within the college and presented as one of the case studies in Chapter 10; Rodney Blunck at the University of Colorado, for his insight into his experience in this area and referral to others who could be of assistance; and Belinda Chavez, who chairs the education division of the American Society for Quality, for her insights and suggestions for directions to take this work.

I would also like to thank Kathy Suerken of the TOC for Education organization for sending me a copy of their TOC for Education workbook which was helpful in preparing the roadmap for achieving educational excellence.

One of the most intriguing discussions I had in developing the concepts in Chapters 6 through 10 was with Kristen Cox from the Office of Management and Budget within the state of Utah. Her explanation and presentation of the state's SUCCESS Framework opened some new directions on how schools could be improved on a daily basis.

The other interesting round of conversations was with the educational professionals at the front lines of educational process improvement in this country. Individuals like Michael Daris with the Tuscaloosa City Schools in Tuscaloosa, Alabama; Jeff Edmondson with StriveTogether who worked with the Covington, Kentucky schools and others; Todd Hoadley with the Dublin School District in Dublin, Ohio; Dr. JoAnn Sternke, the Baldrige Award winner with the Pewaukee, Wisconsin schools; Jim Loyd with the Olmsted Falls schools in Olmstead Falls, Ohio; Andrew True with the Kingsport, Tennessee schools; and Johnny Giles with the Huntsville, Alabama city schools.

I would also like to thank those who contributed to the content of this book: Jeremy Garrett and Matthew Redmond for their material on how they use the tools in their high school classrooms; Dr. Pat Greco and Molly Paulus from the Menomonee Falls School District and Dr. B. J. Worthington and April Sparks from the Clarksville-Montgomery County Schools with the material for the case studies in Chapters 7 and 8.

Finally, I would like to thank Bryan Albrecht, Kamalijit Jackson, Bob Sproull, Loren Murfield, and Carl Nielson for their willingness to review this work and contribute an endorsement of the strategies I have presented.

During my Six Sigma Black Belt training I learned my lessons well and have with some effort found the path to relate them to the educational arena. Despite learning those lessons it was still critical that my efforts be reviewed by independent eyes with the mission to determine whether I got the material across in a manner easily understood by the everyday education professionals. So I thank Rachel Porter, a brand-new teacher starting out in the profession, for her views on the applicability to her career.

I would also be remiss if I did not acknowledge the contribution of two individuals to the journey I have undertaken. Eliyahu Goldratt, who I never had the pleasure of meeting and who left us way too early, through his work *The Goal* and subsequent related titles, started me on this journey. His introduction on how to identify the obstacles in our organizational functions was an eye-opener into some illogical efforts on the part of many organizations. William F. Mazurek, who over the past 3 years has filled the roles of my instructor, my advisor, and my guide through the Six Sigma arena. He is the instructor of the Six Sigma Black Belt program at St. Petersburg College.

This work would not have come to fruition if it were not for the assistance of the staff at Productivity Press including Michael Sinocchi, my editor. Thank you for your time and efforts to bring this message to the educational world.

Cheryl T. Bloom, my wife for over 40 years, who watched me go through the 9-month process of writing my first book and still encouraged me to begin this project.

About the Author

Backed by over 30 years of professional experience as a thought leader in the area of human resources and process improvement along with 6 years in the classroom as a middle school science teacher, Daniel Bloom has assisted organizations of all sizes in the areas of talent acquisition and management, equal employment, workplace investigations, policy design, corporate mobility, and curriculum design.

Since 2006, Daniel Bloom has been a frequent contributor in the social media space via his website, BestThinking.com, the Human Capital League, Recruiting Blogs, Toolbox HR, and others. Further, he has appeared both in print and in online media articles. He is the author of four books in which he has discussed process improvement in a variety of industries. He is the owner of the LinkedIn Group "How to Become the Critical HR Leader You Are Meant to Be" and a member of the Lean Six Sigma in Education group. He holds membership in the Suncoast HR Management Association as well as the American Society for Quality.

Daniel Bloom is a graduate of Parsons College with a degree in education and holds certifications as a Senior Professional in Human Resources (SPHR) and as a Six Sigma Black Belt. He founded Daniel Bloom & Associates Inc. in 1980 following a layoff from the ECI Division of E-Systems.

Introduction

We are facing a crisis in this country. I am not referring to the various talking points brought up by our politicians on both sides of the aisle. I am talking about a crisis within our educational system. I am talking about a system where our children no longer know how to think critically. I am talking about an educational system, which is typically represented by bloated bureaucracies.

In 2007 the National Center on Education and the Economy (NCEE) produced their report *Tough Choices or Tough Times*[1] discussing the American educational system and the challenges it faces in preparing our younger generation for the workplace of tomorrow. I would suggest to the reader that the American educational system is facing far greater challenges from two fronts on a daily basis.

The first front is in the classroom. According to the Center for Budget and Policy Priorities,[2] the various state legislatures have continued to decrease funding for schools:

At least 31 states provided less state funding per student in the 2014 school year (that is, the school year ending in 2014) than in the 2008 school year, before the recession took hold. In at least 15 states, the cuts exceeded 10%.

In at least 18 states, *local* government funding per student fell over the same period. In at least 27 states, local funding rose, but those increases rarely made up for cuts in state support. Total local funding nationally—for the states where comparable data exists—*declined* between 2008 and 2014, adding to the damage from state funding cuts.

While data on total school funding in the *current* school year (2016) is not yet available, at least 25 states are still providing less "general" or "formula" funding—the primary form of state funding for schools—per student than in 2008. In seven states, the cuts exceed 10%.

Along with the reduced funding for the schools, society demands a certain level of performance, and these demands are often centered in contrived metrics designed to demonstrate the level of performance in the classroom.

The second front is the amount of waste in the operation side of the schools. One local school district just received a consultant's report indicating that they had over the years hired too many staff.[3] If we search, there are many other examples of such waste in our schools today.

The purpose of the book you are holding in your hands at the moment is to suggest that there is a different way to approach these problems. The world we are living in is facing a lot of uncertainty brought on by change. Our seasons change. Our weather undergoes changes. We get older (forgot I was not supposed to remind the reader of that). These are changes over which we, as individuals, have no control. They just happen, whether we are actively involved in the change or a passive onlooker. Every day, nature undergoes change to some degree.

Our response to these changes will determine whether our schools survive or cease to function. Since I entered the classroom in the late 1960s, there has been a dramatic shift in the way we look at education and its roles. While the demands have changed, many of the operating ways have not, creating major issues for the schools as they try and resolve the issues discussed in the aforementioned NCEE report. In fact, the changes may carry heavier penalties for non-action than the rest of the global hierarchy. We can no longer function as an antiquated silo unto ourselves. The period of functioning silos has gone the same way as the eight-track cassette (I think I finally got rid of my remaining ones recently). These changes have brought education to a vital crossroads requiring very difficult decisions on the part of both education and management as a whole.

Stop for a moment and close your eyes. Imagine you are driving down this lonely stretch of road and find yourself facing a fork in the road. Think about the following question before you answer; which fork are you going to take? More important, why did you take the path you did? Understand that your decision carries direct outcomes for your school and your future. Let's consider your alternatives.

The left fork represents the easy route. Both the administration and classroom professionals along with the community as a whole are complacent with the way things are now. We see bloated administrative staffs with the tendency to overlook redundancies. We see classroom human capital assets who are content in sending the message that it is "my way or no way." We find procurement personnel who select vendors based on other factors than whether the vendor can deliver their products and/or services effectively and efficiently within a school budget. You have a new solution to a problem, but you have to send it through the chain of command. You need to change your curriculum, but you have to go see the department head or the principal. You need a policy police for the organization, go see the principal. The problem is that the real message you send is that at the same time you are telling the organization that you are open to change, you are also telling them that you are content working in a state of mediocrity and rapidly becoming a commodity. Where is the justification for the value of your position to the organization? This feeling comes from a view that you are operating at maximum effort and that your educational processes have no room for improvement. I can remember back to the late 1970s when I was teaching science in a private school in New York City and was told I had to change the way I was teaching science because the principal knew how to teach science since she had done so 25 years earlier.

The right fork is an uncomfortable path. It is a path in which you are forced to challenge the entire process. By the entire process I mean both inside the classroom and outside the classroom. By the entire process I mean new ways to present the curriculum. By the entire process I mean how the functional side of the institution works. In what manner do we run the school? This uncomfortable path applies to all educational institutions, public or private. It applies to Pre-K as well as our universities. It applies to the public and private schools as well as hybrids of these. As educational professionals, you are embarking on a journey that will get you out of your comfort zone. You have been arguing until you are blue in the face that you want to be part of the strategic decisions within your school, but you have not to this point demonstrated the supporting evidence to put you there. You have moved from being part of the problem to being part of the solution in responding to the changing market conditions as they affect your organization.

This book serves a dual purpose. This book is going to take you on a journey that will lay out the path to resolve these feelings of uncertainty.

The first purpose is to provide the educational professional with the evidence to present to the administration that you belong at the table. In your role as part of the educational system, you play a substantial role in the success of the school. It shows you as the educational professional how to develop metrics that are creditable, verifiable, and appropriate for the circumstances that you are working in.

The second purpose is to vastly improve the entire educational system by providing the vehicle to run the organization faster, cheaper, and better. How do we change our systems and policies to deliver them to the school quicker, at less cost, and without errors?

In the pages that follow, I have laid out a roadmap to take you through the journey I have described. The ultimate goal is to lay out a method that has been used by educational organizations of various sizes and industries worldwide. It is difficult to explain where you are headed without a clear picture of where we have been. So we will start at the beginning, with a look at the history of the quality movement, and complete the journey with a look at the future. As a result, the chapters that follow are laid out in the same logical progression. The ultimate outcome will be the ability to demonstrate to the stakeholders within your organization that you have reached a state of educational excellence.

In Chapter 1, we will define What Do We Mean by Educational Excellence? Trying to determine a basic definition of excellence is as difficult as trying to determine what is beautiful. We will try and arrive at a definition of the term excellence from both an organizational perspective and, equally, as a part of the strategic objectives of the educational space. The intent is to develop a clear picture as to what our ultimate goal is.

In Chapter 2, "Where Did Six Sigma Come From?," we take a look at where we have been. We review the various evolutionary steps that the total quality movement has undergone as we have reached where we are today. On an equal basis, the roadmap reviews both the successes and the failures of the past 50-plus years since the continuous process improvement efforts began.

In Chapter 3, we begin to explore "Six Sigma What Is It?" You will discover the basic tenets of the problem-solving method. We will look at the impact on an elementary level regarding the principles that govern how we implement the changes to our organizations. Also considered are the roles within project management along with the requisite training and when the utilization of Six Sigma is best practice within the organization.

In Chapter 4, "Six Sigma Toolbox," we begin our deep dive into the Six Sigma methodology by reviewing the method from the creation of a project to its successful completion. At each stage, we look at the precise tools that are available for your consideration. Some of the examples of the tools will be accompanied with actual educational related examples. Another aspect of the chapter will be a discussion of QI Macros, which is an Excel-based add-on created by KnowledgeWare of Denver, Colorado.[4]

Chapter 5, "In Plain Sight: Sources of Wastes," explores the fact that every process has its hiccups that cause the process to break down, sometimes slightly, sometimes dramatically. When the hiccups are hidden they have a tendency to come back to bite the organization. These hiccups are hidden because the organization has never looked for them. The continuous process improvement recognizes nine different types of non-value-added activities that are in existence in most organizations. In reviewing the nine types of waste, we will begin to relate the process directly to education by looking at real-time examples of waste within the classroom space.

Chapter 6, "Applied Six Sigma and the Classroom," begins our journey through the role of Six Sigma within the educational arena. The content of this chapter looks at scenarios where schools of a wide selection of types and locations have introduced the process into the classroom.

In Chapter 7, we carry the Applied Six Sigma and the Classroom into the operation side of the equation with a review of how the methodology has been applied to the way we run our schools.

In Chapter 8, we try and bring all the various strategies we have discussed to transform your organization into a Lean Six Sigma principled one. It lays out a hierarchy of the exact steps to achieve the goal.

In Chapter 9, I provide you with some strategies to begin to implement the processes I have discussed in your schools with suggestions for easily implemented steps.

In the final chapter, we revisit our definition of educational excellence and suggest some very concrete strategies to achieve educational excellence in this new world we have designed.

As a supplement, I have provided you with some Further Reading titles to assist you if you want to enhance the knowledge you have gained from this work.

Let's begin the journey.

Notes

1. National Center on Education and the Economy. *Tough Choices or Tough Times*. San Francisco, CA: Jossey-Bass, 2007
2. Center for Budget and Policy Priorities. http://www.cbpp.org/research/state-budget-and-tax/most-states-have-cut-school-funding-and-some-continue-cutting. January 2016.

3. Marlene Sokol. Consultant advises Hillsborough School District to shed more than 1700 jobs. *Tampa Bay Times*. June 1, 2016.
4. QI Macros is an Excel-based collection of Six Sigma tools that is developed by KnowledgeWare. For more information visit http://www.qimacros.com.

Chapter 1

What Do We Mean by Educational Excellence?

This third installment in the *Achieving Excellence through Six Sigma* series is still concerned with the language of business. Like the previous titles,[1] it is crucial that we begin by establishing as much as possible a definitive idea of what we believe the definition of excellence is. Further, we need to establish what we mean then by the term educational excellence. You are a corporate executive being transferred to a new location, and one of the first questions you propose is "where are the excellent schools?" The problem is, what do you mean by the concept excellent schools?

Have you ever watched a jaywalking segment on *The Tonight Show*? I am not referring to the act of crossing the street in the middle of the block. I am referring to Jay Leno going out on the streets of Hollywood and asking everyday people a specific question on any number of topics. Suffice to say that some of the answers are in the range from correct to bizarre. Try a jaywalking type exercise, but ask the people you approach to define the concept of *excellence*. I guarantee that you will receive a wide variety of answers as excellence is in the eyes of the beholder. Responses will be guided by the biases and cultural upbringing that have shaped your growth as a human being. But it does point out a fact of human nature. In almost everything we do, our ultimate goal is to reach as close to a state of perfection as is possible. If in doubt, consider the examples in Figure 1.1.

You have lived in this global environment, and as such your environment has generated certain feelings toward what is excellent and what is not. Your environment pressures you to answer the question in a particular way or

Bowling – A score of 300 knocking down all the pins

Golf – Hitting that hole in one

Baseball – No hitter

Business - Reach a level of 99.99966% defect free

Figure 1.1 States of perfection.

fashion. These biases influence everything you do and say. From a personal perspective, each person is going to have a concept in mind that defines excellence.

Our schools are no different. In education, every school or school system is trying to reach the optimum performance level for their stakeholders. The difficulty is that they are serving dual constituents. Each will have their own definition of excellence. The student population is seeking a curriculum that meets their needs for the future. Does the curriculum empower them to be able to obtain the employment they want for the post-graduation era? The taxpayers are seeking a school system which is not overspending their tax dollars. They both are seeking the ability to say that we excel at what we do. The difficulty, however, is that the definition of excellence is allusive in nature.

In supporting what I am suggesting, open your Web browser and Google the "*definition of excellence*," and the results will tell you the difficulty we have in arriving at a concrete definition. A Google search for the "*definition of excellence*" returns 54,300,000 results. If I change the search parameters to "*defining excellence*," the number drops to 49,800,000. If I take it one step further and Google "*defining educational excellence*," it returns 3,580,000 results. The dilemma is that being confronted with this wide assortment of definitions, as individuals, we have a hard time determining a single definition for excellence that everyone can settle upon. One way to make that determination is to recognize that there are certain conditions that must be present for us to even begin to talk of excellence.

I discussed previously about the wide variety of definitions found on Google. The *Merriam-Webster Dictionary*,[2] one of the oldest and most well-known dictionaries, defines excellence as being a noun, which shows an excellent or valuable quality. It also means setting a high standard. So, if we follow the logic from *Merriam-Webster*, we begin to see that excellence means that we need to demonstrate that we are operating at a level perceived to be the best of class compared to our peers in terms of what our responsibility levels are supposed to be.

Another discussion of the definition of excellence takes us to the Moral Learning blog.[3] The owner of the blog indicates he found a great biblical verse that in his perspective defines excellence. He turned to the book of Genesis 26:13, which states

> *"The man became great. He continued becoming greater until he was exceedingly great."*

The first characteristic of the term excellence is that there is no finishing or end point. It is not finite in time. Like what we will be discussing later in the book, we need to continuously strive to be the best at what we do. We need to strive to reach that point where we can tell the world that we excel at what we do. This means that as conditions change, so do the conditions required to reach a point of excellence. It calls for us to reach to new levels as the conditions change.

Jeffrey Spear, president of Studio Spear, in an article for the American Marketing Association entitled "Defining Excellence,"[4] suggested that trying to reach this point of consensus is totally subjective, adding to our difficulties in our endeavors. He also suggests that in a real sense excellence is something we have created to attach value to the things we create and validate our choices.

Reportedly, if you visit the US Military Academy at West Point, you will find engraved on the wall of the one of the buildings the definition shown in Figure 1.2.

The quote suggests that to reach a point of excellence we have to invest more of ourselves so as to reach the best indicated by our ultimate goal.

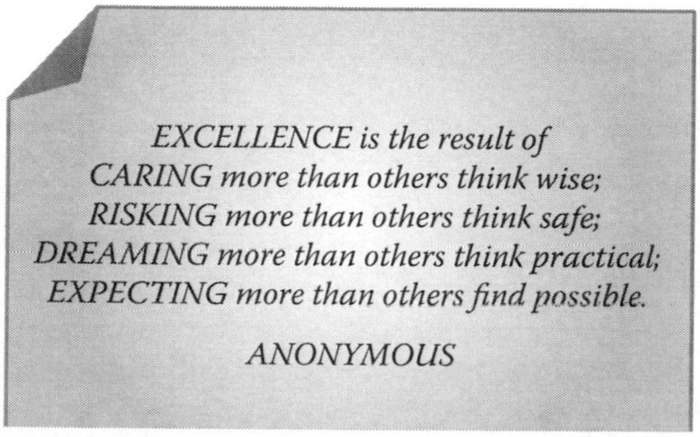

> *EXCELLENCE is the result of*
> *CARING more than others think wise;*
> *RISKING more than others think safe;*
> *DREAMING more than others think practical;*
> *EXPECTING more than others find possible.*
>
> *ANONYMOUS*

Figure 1.2 Anonymous quote.

The West Point definition suggests that excellence is a set of behaviors or actions that manifest themselves in the way we are perceived, by those who influence us. It suggests that to achieve a state of excellence we are required to change from the path of least resistance (the left fork I discussed in the introduction to this book) to more involvement in the outcomes (the right fork in the same discussion). The changes are required both as an individual and as an educational institution. It further suggests that to achieve a state of excellence you have to be an active participant in the change process.

Obviously, I could go on forever talking about a wide variety of definitions for the term excellence and try to create a generic definition in the long run; however, it would not resolve the central question of this text, which is how do we reach the near perfection level of best in class? Understand that every process within your school has its hiccups, and it is the hidden ones that come back to bite. Excellence can be achieved when our organizational resources are directed toward a series of actions that include the following.

The Acquisition and Integration of Passionate and Culturally Aligned Human Capital Assets That Are Engaged and Aligned with the School's Goals

Excellence needs to be imbedded in the total organization. From an educational perspective, you need the involvement of the teachers in the classroom as well as the support staff. To achieve our goal of educational excellence, your organization needs to actively seek out individuals who are passionate and aligned with these educational goals. In addition, these acquired human capital assets must actively participate in a cross-functional team approach in resolving the issues regarding less-than-stellar operations of the school. The efforts of the school personnel must be aligned with the mission of the school as they deliver the products and services to the stakeholders.

Using Tools and Processes to Advance the Educational Mission

Whether they are on a formal basis or created ad hoc, every function within the organization has its share of tools and the processes that are utilized to reportedly make the silo function run more efficiently. The difficulty has been that these tools and processes are not based on a complete understanding of the overall educational organization.

To reach a state of educational excellence, the tools and processes that are utilized in the school need to be completely aligned with the total school. The instructional staff and the administration need to understand what the ultimate goals of the educational system are and how their tools and processes assist the school in reaching the organization's mission, strategy, and goals.

The Focus on Elements That Are Strategic, Transactional, and Compliance Issues

Instructional and administrative sides of the coin have a role within the educational organization, whether we are talking about the new view or the old one, but the question is, what is the focus of that effort? If it is centered on educational excellence, we need to change the focus to whether every action is undertaken from the perspective that what we do enhances the strategic and transactional processes. Not everything we do as educational professionals is value added. To reach educational excellence, we need to redirect the magnifying glass to what is important in our decisions on the ultimate strategy of the school.

There are voices from all sorts of streams of thought that seem to have a never-ending list of ideas on how to improve our schools. Ranging from a more testing to a common curriculum, they express the intent to make mainly the classroom professional responsible for the educational excellence in our schools. There is never a mention of changing the processes involved; instead we are expected to change the tools.

The Focus on Gaining and Maintaining a Seat at the Table

The Theory of Constraints–Lean–Six Sigma (TLS) Continuum and the effort toward educational excellence only occur when we work as a cross-functional team. The voices we often hear usually apply to those in the classroom, not the administration. We can only reach our stated goal of educational excellence when we work as a total effort with each sitting at the table to solve our problems together.

The Securing, Training, and Retaining of Talent to Meet the Corporate Educational Strategies

I talked earlier about the West Point quote and its demands on excellence. If we are going to reach the state of educational excellence then we need to change the entire educational organization. This change does not come from doing things the same way you have always done and expecting the change to naturally happen. It will require changes in behavior for it to occur. *Educational Leadership*, the journal of the American Society for Curriculum Development, published an article titled "Excellence for All," written by Robert J. Sternberg, in which the author discussed four models for defining excellence.[5] Sternberg suggests that the models look at the educational institution only at the bottom of the school, look only at the top, look only at the middle, and last, look only at the statistical advantage. The problem is each of these models leaves out a part of the greater organization.

One of the ways to bring about this organizational change is to implement training to demonstrate why the change is necessary to the sustainability of the school organization.

This change will be brought about by philosophy about a way of operating. To be successful going forward, the educational institution needs to move from functional silos to a cross-functional model. Every one of our decisions needs to be centered on what is good for the entire organization, not the classroom for example. We are going to need to train both current and future human capital assets on the purpose and intent of the changes. We are going to need to create and put in place a standardized training process for new talent assets. Jeffrey Liker, in his book *Toyota Culture*[6] and his follow up, *Toyota Talent*,[7] demonstrates a clear picture of the process used in the Toyota Production System to orient the internal and external human capital assets to the new corporate philosophy.

It has been said that if you search long enough, you can find support for just about any view on the Web. When I did, I found the vast majority of the Google search results were all student centric at the expense of the administrative side. I also found, interestingly, that the Baldrige National Quality Program, which many corporations are familiar with, has an educational component.[8] The Baldrige Educational Framework in part follows the manufacturing side of the program.

Organizational aspects
- *P1: Organizational description*
- *P2: Organizational situation*

Leadership
- *1.1 Senior leadership*
- *1.2 Governance and societal responsibilities*

Strategy
- *2.1 Strategy development*
- *2.2 Strategy implementation*

Customer
- *3.1 Voice of the customer*
- *3.2 Customer engagement*

Measurement, analysis, and improvement
- *4.1 Measurement, analysis, and improvement of organizational performance*
- *4.2 Knowledge management, information, and information technology*

Workforce
- *5.1 Workforce environment*
- *5.2 Workforce engagement*

Operations
- *6.1 Work processes*
- *6.2 Operational effectiveness*

Results
- *7.1 Student learning and process results*
- *7.2 Customer-focused results*
- *7.3 Workforce-focused results*
- *7.4 Leadership and governance results*
- *7.5 Budgetary, financial, and market results*

The readers are directed toward the Baldrige Educational Framework website. At the same time as shown previously, the criteria are not centered just on the student output or the organizational output. The award criteria provide the evidence that excellence is seen from the total organization.

With that in mind, I thought that it was important to get the input of fellow educational practitioners as to what they thought the concept of educational excellence means. I posted on LinkedIn questions and answers concerning "What is educational excellence?" Over a 5-day time span I received three responses. What was interesting about the responses was that they were all one-sided in their approach to educational excellence. Without exception, they reported that the definition of educational excellence was centered on the process outputs from the perception of the student. They also used almost the same wording such as "educational excellence provides choices that enable and encourage an individual to capitalize on his or her strengths rather than compensate them for weaknesses." The problem here is that it leaves out the other side of the educational institution.

Of these responses, only one individual reported back that I should turn my efforts back to administration and not worry about the other aspects. The single response that suggested we should remain focused on the administrative responsibilities represents the left fork in our scenario. It represents the path of least resistance. It is the path that Human Resources have always taken. It is a path from which we placed ourselves in this silo, if you will. Here are Human Resources. So what if there are operational issues, we don't have to worry about them because it is not our job or in our position duties. We are an entity unto ourselves and based on what we do. As a result, management considered us to be a necessary evil within the organization. You have hiring managers who feel they can do a better job and so circumvent Human Resources at every opportunity.

The majority of the people I talked to found it really hard to provide a solid response to the question. This was due to the nature of the fact that the definition can be very situational specific. Their answers are very much centered on the organizational culture and goals. Since these characteristics are organizational specific, the resulting definition may vary to some degree.

Based on this evidential information presented in the preceding paragraphs, I can now establish what I believe is a basic definition of educational excellence, which is central to this book. To me, educational excellence means that we begin with the acknowledgment that education will now be judged on the basis of what we deliver[9] to the stakeholders strategically. It is our effort to demonstrate that we are not just this silo within the organization who confines their purview to a single piece of the pie. More important, it plans out a series of actions that makes us become totally involved in the internal and external processes of the organization. It means that to achieve educational excellence, professionals must be actively involved within the continuous process improvement effort throughout the organization.

Educational excellence means that we are able to define what education is in terms of the financial impact of the organization decisions. As we strive to improve the organizational processes based on the strategic objectives, we need to constantly keep in mind how we can deliver these efforts faster, better, and cheaper. We need to be able to show the rate of improvement and how the changes have increased the bottom line of the total organization.

It means that we are able to deliver creditable, verifiable data-based metrics to provide stakeholders with a clear picture of what we are providing to the organization and the community. The metrics must be able to describe in understandable terms where we were and where we are going. The data collected must be directly attributable to the problem at hand.

Do We Know What to Work on Next?

The continuous process improvement effort is a never-ending process within any organization. However, that does not mean we can do everything at once. Educational excellence means that we have the ability to look at the organization and choose the few best opportunities for improving the organization.

Where Is the Educational Excellence Going to Take Us?

The second question asks that we take into consideration where achieving educational excellence will take us. We need to understand not only where we are but what we will look like when we get there. Our efforts to improve the education must have a clear picture of both current and future states and what it means to the organization as a whole.

If our desire is to reach a true state of educational excellence, I believe we don't have a choice to remain in the status quo. If you determine that you want to reach the state of educational excellence then there some very succinct steps we must take. First, education professionals must look at the way they operate and identify the ways that we impede the success of the organization. We have to do this not only through a different attitude but through a changed direction. Educational excellence demands that we look at each and every thing we do through the lens of the total organization, not the instructional or administrative silo. Second, educational excellence will require that the school be able to explain in clear terms why we have a larger role to play within the community. It is only then that we can achieve the scenario dictated by this definition. Achieving educational excellence is your choice. It is your choice to determine that you are taking the right steps toward a new role for education within your communities.

In the chapters that follow I will create the roadmap that will allow us to reach this point. I will be able to show what we need to work on, what is not adding value to the stakeholders (both internal and external), and how to improve the process so that stakeholders are getting their money's worth from our schools, and finally, I will be able in concrete terms to describe what the ultimate organization looks like and why we have a critical part in that perspective. In the final chapter of this book, I take you on a roadmap with specific steps to reach our ultimate goal.

Notes

1. *Achieving HR Excellence through Six Sigma* (2013) and *The Field Guide to Achieving HR Excellence through Six Sigma* (2016).
2. *Encyclopedia Britannica*. Definition of Excellence. http://www.merriam-webster.com/dictionary/excellence. 2011.
3. Moral Learning blog. http://morallearning.blogspot.com/2007/06/definition-of-excellence.html. 2007.
4. Spear, Jeffrey. "Defining Excellence." http://www.studiospear.com/downloads/DefiningExcellence.pdf.
5. Sternberg, Robert J. *Excellence for All*. Educational Leadership. October 2008. http://www.ascd.org/publications/educationalleadership/oct08/num02/excellence-for-all/aspx.
6. Liker, Jeffrey. *Toyota Culture*. New York: McGraw-Hill, 2008.
7. Liker, Jeffrey. *Toyota Talent*. New York: McGraw-Hill, 2007.
8. Baldrige National Quality Program Educational program. https://www.nist.gov/baldrige/about-baldrige-excellence-framework-education.
9. For more information on this change of focus, the readers are referred to the works of David Ulrich, especially in his book *HR Transformation*.

Chapter 2

Where Did Six Sigma Come From?

Introduction

In the previous chapter, I strived to find common ground on what a working definition would be for educational excellence. With that definition in mind, from Chapter 2 and continuing to the last chapter, I will carry that definition throughout the remainder of this book. The journey unfolds in logical steps, so that you can obtain a clear understanding of the concepts presented.

Like most journeys, you have to have a starting point, and so Chapter 2 is devoted to discovering where we have been and the methodologies that are available to us going forward. Chapter 3 will discuss what Six Sigma is. Chapters 4 through 6 take us through a look at the responsibilities of the cross-functional teams, the project types, and the circumstances where Six Sigma is appropriate to be utilized.

While the general timeline of the evolution of Total Quality Management (TQM) is followed, I do not intend this chapter to be a treatise on the TQM process or its evolution, but rather a very basic introduction to provide you with the foundation for the rest of the journey. My intended purpose is not to write a history of the quality movement as this has been done earlier, in the writings of Goldratt,[1] Liker,[2] Pande,[3] and others.

Toyota Production System

The Toyota Production System (TPS) was created over a quarter of a century (1945), resulting in a system that is as much a continuous process improvement effort as a way to create a new cultural model. It is designed to create a new framework in which the company operates based on the agricultural era of Japan. Its primary objective[4] was to eliminate work that was overburdening the workforce. At the same time, the company strived to remove inconsistency and eliminate waste. This was the beginning of the Lean movement in the process improvement area.

There are several important points that the TPS put in place that have a direct bearing on the discussion in the final chapter of this book regarding how we achieve educational excellence. First, the basis for determining success is less about the people involved and more about the way the process operates. Many organizations today are convinced that the solution to problems in the organization is to reduce the head count. The problem is that organizations will tend to cut some of their best human capital assets without solving the problem. This road to educational excellence is never about the people involved.

The second point is that of a consideration of the standard of work. Educational excellence is not about removing creativity and innovation from the educational organization. What it is about is identifying a process and maintaining a definitive step-by-step system for performing the process. The key to the effort is to identify a standard method for solving the school problems. I could go on for some time about the system, but as mentioned previously the Liker books provide a thorough review of the TPS. Liker's treatment is far more to the point of the inner workings of the system. The role here is to present the various perspectives that led to the introduction of Six Sigma as it is used today in the Theory of Constraints–Lean–Six Sigma (TLS) Continuum.

Quality Circles

Following World War II, the individuals behind the Japanese efforts to resurrect their businesses began to look at ways to improve the workplace. Kaoru Ishikawa created one of these developments called quality circles.

The first organization to utilize quality circles was Nippon Wireless and Telegraph, starting about 1962. Quality circles functioned essentially the same, regardless of the organizational structure.

The concept behind the operation of quality circles was that they were comprised of small groups of managers and employees who voluntarily got together to solve intercompany problems. The members were trained in the tenets of statistical process control, giving them the basis for identifying and analyzing processes within the organization. The meetings were held around the normal work schedule, occurring either during lunch breaks or before or after work. It should be noted that solutions were designed to handle issues ranging from safety and health to product design and manufacturing process improvements, so we are not talking about large-scale problems. Further, despite the principle set for W. Edwards Deming, the circles were more than likely within the same department or silo. Once a solution was developed, it was presented to management for permission to implement the steps to change the process. After gaining management approval, the solution was implemented. In some cases, the members of the quality circle were awarded bonuses based on the amount of savings generated by their solutions. A simple overview of their operation is shown next.

HUMAN RESOURCE EXCELLENCE 101: QUALITY CIRCLES

Mary Johnson has been a member of the human resource function at Excellence Manufacturing for nearly 15 years. One day she is reviewing an e-mail from a department manager, in which they are lamenting about the length of time it takes to obtain approval for a new hire to take place. Mary talks with both the manager and some of her fellow department members to determine where the process is breaking down.

Based on the conversations, the people directly involved decide they will try and improve the process. The team consists of Mary, two of her fellow Human Resources (HR) team members, and the department manager. They begin to meet once a week after hours looking at the current process. From their review they identify what the problems are, select the final issue that needs to be resolved, and analyze the impact of the problem on overall operations.

Following the completion of their studies, they compile a report on the problem that was identified and the recommended solution and present their report to the organizational management team. Management, after the review of the completed project, gives the team the go ahead to implement the solution.

Their solution decreased the new hire approval process, saving the organization approximately $100,000 in cost reductions. In turn, the quality circle members received a 2% bonus in their pay to reward their efforts.

In 1972, based on the success of quality circles in Japan, the improvement staff of the Lockheed Space Missile Factory in California brought these circles to the United States. Japanese organizations demonstrated that the circles brought major changes in their organizations. The interest came about after aerospace representatives visited an assortment of Japanese manufacturing facilities and saw the quality circles in operation.[5]

The use of quality circles continued until 1990, when the National Labor Relations Board (NLRB) intervened. The NLRB determined that certain quality circles called labor-management committees were a violation of the Wagner Act. Signed by Franklin Delano Roosevelt in 1935, the purpose of the legislation was to guarantee the right of employees to join a union or labor organizations through an organization of their choosing. In a case involving Electromation Incorporated, the NLRB determined that the firm established the quality circles, and the firm determined the agenda. Further, the action management teams (as they were called) addressed the conditions of employment. Several years later, the NLRB issued a similar decision in a case against DuPont Corporation, accusing DuPont of using quality circles to circumvent the union–management negotiations.

Faced with the potential for legal challenges, by the end of the 1900s the use of quality circles in the United States had dwindled substantially.

Total Quality Management

Despite the efforts of Deming, Ishikawa, and others, not everyone was enthralled with this thing called the quality movement. Not every organization was excited about the potential for quality circles and their potential obstacles. These corporations looking for something new in 1968 began a movement that became known as TQM.

Unlike quality circles, TQM returned to the ideas of Deming and others and structured its principle around the 14 points of quality discussed later in this chapter. To achieve this, TQM looked at both the quality of the products that were produced and the reduction of variations in the internal processes.

TQM does not have a universal introduction process; however, it proved to be more effective than quality circles. Contrary to quality circles, the efforts to improve the organizational process were introduced to the total organization. We no longer consider the silos but rather how each of the identified problems impacts the total organization. Total Quality Engineering on its website[6] introduces a simple model to understand the impact of TQM on the efforts to remove non-value-added activities from within the organization.

The process begins with gaining a clear understanding of the wants and needs of the customer. What is it that the customers really need? What are the customers willing and able to pay to make their lives easier in the long run? The view of customer needs relies on the customer obtaining the products or services they need, when they need them, at a value that meets their needs. As discussed further in the review of the Six Sigma methodology, the perspective of our organizations from the way the customer sees it is critical to our meeting the continuous process improvement efforts. There is a wide range of vehicles to obtain this information.

Once an organization has gained a clear picture of customer needs, these needs are integrated into the planning process. It is important to stress here that standardized work is emphasized further in this book. At this point, it is sufficient to say that whenever an internal process deviates from the expectations of a customer regarding the delivery process, there is a deviation from the standard work. It also critical that as customer needs are introduced into the various internal processes, it is also necessary to manage the processes to ensure that the customer experience is the basis for any and all process improvement.

Again, as discussed further in this book, the next step after introducing the customer needs into the planning process is to analyze the points where we are creating non-value-added waste in the process and see where to act and what we have to do to bring the process back within the standard work model. The ultimate goal is to remove the non-value-added efforts so the process is as close to the point of perfection as possible.

The final stage in the Total Quality Engineering model is that of total participation. As demonstrated by such organizations as General Electric (GE) and others, the mission or value statement was that the sense of improving the organization to meet the customer needs had to be organization-wide. It also led to a review regarding whether these customer wants or needs were in alignment with the organizational strategic objectives. This meant that every function within the organization from the superintendent of schools to the classroom teacher to the front office had to be included in the effort to satisfy the customer wants. The creation of cross-functional teams was intended to assist the organization in making continuous process improvement a piece of the organizational culture.

Motorola

In 1986, a scientist at Motorola had been studying the TPS and was intrigued by the outcomes. He was in need of a method for describing the number of defects found in a particular process. Bill Smith created what we now know as Six Sigma. If any organization holds the rights to the concept it is Motorola.

From its inception, it has evolved as the concept moved out into the work environment. About 9 years later, GE brought it into their organization as the next step in improving the workout process and the change acceleration process (CAP). GE likewise created its own internal system and provided unique training in this area to the entire organization.

Earlier I mentioned the work of Larry Bossidy within the CAP model. Bossidy eventually left the GE organization and became the chief executive officer (CEO) of a company called Allied Signal (which later merged with and became known as Honeywell), the large electronic firm. Bossidy took what he viewed as the best of the Motorola system and the best of the GE system and merged them into a new model, which he spread throughout Honeywell. Having done so, he saw both productivity and removal waste occur in big numbers.

DEMING'S 14 POINTS OF QUALITY

1. Create constancy of purpose for improvement of products and services.
2. Adapt the new philosophy.
3. Cease dependence on mass inspection.

4. End the practice of awarding business on price tag only.
5. Improve constantly and forever the system of production and service.
6. Institute training.
7. Institute leadership.
8. Drive out fear.
9. Break down barriers between staff areas.
10. Eliminate slogans, exhortations, and targets for the workforce.
11. Eliminate numerical quotas.
12. Remove the barriers to pride of workmanship.
13. Institute a vigorous program of education and retraining.
14. Take action to accomplish the transformation.

Deming's 14 Points of Quality

Credited with being the father of process improvement, Deming taught both American and Japanese corporations how to improve their processes. There have been and could be whole books devoted to Deming and his philosophy toward business processes. They are better suited to describing his works than the purpose of this book allows. I will, however, take some time to consider Deming's 14 Points of Quality which was the basis of his efforts.

Deming's 14 Points of Quality can be found in an article on Wikipedia, which discusses the points in some detail.[7] To understand the path that TQM took, we need to understand what Deming was suggesting. To obtain that footing, if you will, let's examine the 14 points a little more in depth.

Create consistency of purpose for improvement of products and services:
One of Deming's Points of Quality is that we approach the concept of quality with a single goal in mind. It makes no difference whether we are dealing with a process that makes something or a process that ends in the provision of a service, the basis is the same. What is our intended destination once we reach our goal? Our purpose must be to identify the non-value-added waste within our organizational operations and remove it. The basis of this purpose is that while the results are important, there is a more important aspect of the methodology. Liker in his book on *Toyota Culture*[8] stresses that what is important to Toyota is not the end results, but rather the problem-solving steps we take to get there. This consistency of purpose that Deming speaks of is based on

this view. Consistency of purpose means that we have to be willing to challenge the status quo every day. We need to understand that every process has its hiccups. It is a natural condition of reality in any organization. Within the educational arena, these hiccups may mean errors in the way we do things.

Adapt the new philosophy: How many times have you tried to implement some changes within the school only to be told "that is not the way we do things around here." Do not feel bad, it happens in virtually every organization globally, no matter what size of operation they have. If we are going to reach that point of educational excellence we discussed in Chapter 1, we need to change our outlook as to the way we operate as an organization. We have to recognize that we are either part of the problem, or we are part of the solution. If we want to be part of the solution, it means we need to change the way we do things for the sake of the very survival of the organization.

Cease dependence on mass inspections: We must not, and more importantly, cannot determine how we are performing by looking at the operations as a whole and saying they are fine. We can't say "hey we are hiring the people we need to, so what is the problem?" We need to look at each process in detail and follow the money if we are to process success. Toyota trains its managers in part by putting them through the circle exercise.[9] The process asks team members to stand in a circle and really observe what is going on.

End the practice of awarding business on the base of price tag: Look, I totally get it. I understand that every management team in the world is looking to maximize the dollars within the organization. I understand that the tendency is to buy as inexpensively as possible. But what if the problem here is that the lowest cost provider does not have the capability of meeting the needs of the customer? Are you still going to use them? I would think not. Instead of working off price point competitiveness, we need to change focus on who can do the best job in delivering on the needs of our customers. The key to reaching educational excellence is not to figure what is best for the organization based on how cheap we can find it. In the context of our ultimate goal this means that we can present our efforts over time as costing less to the organization in terms of non-value-added steps being removed. We will consider this point in more detail in later chapters.

Improve constantly and forever the system of production and service: There is not a single process within any organization worldwide that is perfect. This new world we are proposing requires us to consistently and constantly look for the better way to perform as an organization. The voice of the customer changes as the work environment changes. We, in turn, need to change our processes to comply with the customer's requests. Deming stated that to reach the quality level we seek we must improve the system.

Institute training: I would not expect that if you were to find out that you were in need of a heart transplant that you would ask your general practitioner to perform the operation. Business is no different.

Our ultimate goal is to reach the point where our human resource operation is considered the best in class, so we need to obtain buy-in from both the management and our fellow employees. The best way to reach this is through providing explicit training for the entire organization. The training needs to look at what we are doing, why we are doing it, and where the organization will be following the training. The training also needs to demonstrate what the organization will look like when we are finished with this segment of the process. The outcome that is sought is that the human capital assets doing the work know (a) how to complete the process and (b) how to complete the process without any intentional errors.

Institute leadership: If you want your organization to reach educational excellence you are confronted with two paths, somewhat different than described earlier. One path is that the educational management of the organization can tell the full-time employees (FTEs) within your organization that we are making the change and they will live with it. The other path is that as the manager expecting the organization to reach educational excellence, can walk the walk and talk the talk. You can demonstrate that you are willing to dive into the change process along with everyone else within the organization. You as the lead toward excellence must show that you are willing to share in the sacrifices that might be required. The message that needs to be delivered is that the management of the organization is able to identify those aspects of the organization that need help using the creditable, verifiable metrics to demonstrate that we are meeting the strategic objectives of the organization.

Drive out fear: Take a page out of Taiichi Ohno's book and look at his "Stand in the Circle" exercise.[10] In doing that, you will find that many organizations operate from an authoritarian view of the organization. If someone makes a mistake it is the employee's fault. The result is that the employee becomes afraid to make a suggestion for FEAR that it will have negative effects on their job and career path.

Change is frightful. Change is scary. Change is about developing a problem-solving method that works for your organization. Change is about taking the risk that your suggestions may be in error. What Deming was suggesting in his Points of Quality is that the organization view of risk needs to reinvent itself to the point that no one in the organization is afraid to make a mistake. In the TLS Continuum model at the end of the book, we will look at this topic more in depth. Our goal is to identify how we can deliver educational resources to the organization faster, better, and cheaper. Our goal is not to drive fear into the organization by challenging any attempts to change the organization.

Break down barriers between staff areas: Decide now whether you want to bring educational excellence to your organization. If you do not then I suggest you put this book away because that is not my intended outcome for the reader of this work. I firmly believe that the only path to success is to have everyone within the organization on the same page. I firmly believe that the only way to achieve this is to foster the belief within the organization that we are all part of one universe. There is no room for grandstanding and the image that one group is above another. Patrick Lencioni clearly points out the dangers of this philosophy in his book *Silos, Politics and Turf Wars.* [11]

Eliminate slogans, exhortations, and targets for the workforce: Management has always for the most part operated from the belief that the way to motivate employees is to put cash in their pockets. They believed the way to motivate the employee base is with fancy slogans that actually mean very little to the workforce. In most cases that I have observed as part of my work career, the fancy slogans and mandatory targets do not work. The goal of educational excellence is to meet the voice of the customer, not to meet some superficial concept developed by the administration and then placed on the heads of the human capital assets.

Eliminate numerical quotas: I am sure we have all operated with the framework of an organization that told its operations that you needed to reach a certain level of output. I am equally convinced that there have been times that you have wondered where they found these numbers, as they made no sense when you looked at the operations as a whole. To reach our intended level of educational excellence, we need to avoid setting arbitrary expected outcomes. We need to let the methodology identify what the process is telling us and what the anticipated future state of the organization is. Our eventual outcomes must be based on creditable, verifiable results, not some number pulled out of the thin air by management edict.

Remove barriers to pride of workmanship: Every organization believes that there are ways to better meet the needs of the customer. The improvements are usually handed down from the top. Organizations need to come to terms with the idea that the part of the organization that knows best how to improve organizational processes are those who are on the front line of the organization. In reaching for educational excellence we need to recognize this premise and fully engage the entire organization within the effort of identifying the non-value-added wastes within the organization. We need to demonstrate that we value their input. We need to instill within the corporate culture the belief that the rank and file is critical to improvement of the relationships with the customers. Take the time to listen to their observations and their suggestions to improve the processes.

Institute a vigorous program of education and retraining: Once you start down the path of continuous process improvement, understand that it is never ending. This means that your organization will be in a constant state of change. Each and every time you complete a process change, it will call for further training within the organization on why the change is happening and how the change will be implemented. We can't expect automatic acceptance and utilization of the new process without showing the process before and after. This comes from extensive training to introduce the changes to the organization.

Take action to accomplish the transformation: If we look at the business landscape and at our personal lives, we can find countless examples of where we talked the right game but we never walked the walk. Just by management stating that we will change will not make it happen. The Six Sigma methodology we will discuss later in this book requires us to take specific steps to bring about the efforts to remove the non-value-added steps to our processes.

Goldratt's Theory of Constraints

With the introduction of *The Goal*[12] in 1984, Dr. Eliyahu Goldratt created an added set of tools to help us resolve customer needs. As we will see later on, the Theory of Constraints is different from the rest of the

Continuum in that it centers on the use of critical thinking skills to identify what is holding us back from delivering the expectations of the customer. It works primarily at the level of the chain driving our search for
the problems to the weakest point of that chain or the obstacle. With the
use of several tools, it allows us to look at the root cause of the obstacle
through thinking about the impact of the process components. It builds
the process map through the use of logistical processes ending in the
defining of maximum value for a particular customer in terms of why the
obstacle or process constraints deliver less than perfect service to them in
the long term.

Crosby's Four Absolutes of Quality

Designed by Phillip Crosby, the four absolutes of quality reflect 39 years of
experience on factory floors for Martin Marietta and ITT. Dr. Crosby was an
industrial engineer who felt that the process improvement effort could be
refined down to four specific absolutes.

Definition of quality is conformance to requirements: Dr. Crosby believed
that the nature of quality was based in the application of processes in a
precise way. It meant getting the process correct the first time around.
To him the sign that the process was not being delivered correctly
was when we delivered it with errors in the process requirements.
Management's responsibility is to coach the human capital assets to follow the process requirements precisely with no variation.

The system of quality is prevention: You should not do quality checks after
the process but rather put measures in place that ensure that the chain
and the system do not make mistakes in the first place.

Performance standard is zero defects: The customer expects the delivery
of your products or services, which meet their needs without less than
perfect delivery. Crosby based the review of the system process performance on how many times the customer received their orders with no
need to rework the process.

The measurement of quality is the price of nonconformance: If you delivered a product or service to a customer and it did not meet the needs
of the customer, what is the cost of redoing the order to meet those
needs? What is the cost to your stakeholders if you do not provide
adequate systems to prepare the students for a future in the workplace?

Think about the cost of errors in the educational processes from both the instructional and administrative perspective.

Juran Trilogy

One of the early tools used to review organizational processes was the use of time studies for the factory floor. One of the people behind this effort was Joseph Juran, who worked at the Hawthorne Works of Western Electric. Juran felt that there were three methodologies that were required by management to produce the quality that the customer expected.

His first methodology was the use of planning tools. In the use of the planning tools the first task is to definitively identify who your clients are. Once you have identified the customer you lay out the problem-solving step and the implementation steps. All the planning tools are used concurrently by all the pieces in the chain.

Juran felt that once the planning stage was completed the process moved to the control stage in which we define what quality means and how to evaluate the process in real time. The final segment of the control effort is to measure the performance gap between real time and the goals and determine how to remove the gap.

Finally, the organization reaches the breakthrough by using new ideas on how to resolve the problems that the other two stages uncovered. The basis is how we improve the performance of the chain in delivering the end user what they contracted for.

Leap Technology/Rapid Workout

Rapid Workout[13]

Created by the organization Leap Technologies, the Rapid Workout was based on benchmark studies competed on the GE Workout process. One of their key findings, which were substantiated by industry studies, was that continuous process improvement efforts typically failed for several reasons.

The first factor was a lack of commitment from senior management. I have already discussed and will show later in the book that we can only reach a state of HR excellence if the management of the organization buys into the concept we are presenting to them. Some managers get it; others feel that it works for others but not in their organization. We need to remember that upper management drives the culture of the organization, and if they are not ready to support your efforts to improve the HR process, it will be difficult.

The second reason for improvement process failure is the reluctance on the part of middle-level managers to release personnel for either belt positions or team members. Many organizations today still operate from a point of view that the primary concern is that a department meet set goals on productivity. Letting even one person move to another area of the organization may have dire outcomes to meeting those goals. What is missing is the ability of middle managers to see the benefits of running a leaner organization.

The final reason is that the rank and file fear change. They fear the outcomes usually based on misinformation as to what all this change process means to the organization. They are mired in the belief that there is only one way to do things: the way they have always done it. The natural outcome is that where there is fear there is obstruction to anything that might change their world.

The Rapid Workout is based on a different working model for Six Sigma–related projects. It sets up different goals for the process. First, it is based on an increased speed of delivery. Rapid Workout is based on the assumption that the entire improvement process will take 60 days to complete compared to 120–350 days in a true Six Sigma based process. One of the initial points of a Six Sigma project is the requirement that you need to provide training for the team members to understand what they are trying to achieve. This new method is based on what the organization already knows and can bring to the table. In essence, Leap Technologies has removed the requirement for initial training of team members. Like the GE Workout, it is based on making decisions and taking action based on the use of built in tools.

Allied Signal

Allied Signal began to look at the Six Sigma methodology in the early 1990s. At the helm was Larry Bossidy who wrote the book *Execution*. Bossidy was a friend and business acquaintance of Jack Welch from GE. He was also the person who convinced Jack Welch to bring the methodology to the GE organization.

Allied Signal called their process Total Quality Leadership and Total Quality Speed, which created a new way of thinking about work within the country. The model was based on a nine-step process.

The system begins with identifying the opportunities for improving the process and ends with acknowledging the project team and communicating through various methods the results to the stakeholders.

GE Workout[14]

In 1960, a University of Massachusetts trained chemical engineer named Jack Welch joined a company called General Electric. In 1971 he was chosen to be the eighth president and chairman of the board of the organization. From our research, he understood that our organizations were overburdened by bureaucracy and non-value-added parts of the process that had nothing to do with the customer needs. As a result, Jack Welch pushed the operating companies to find ways to improve how they did things. Based on some strategic efforts he put in place, the value of the organization increased 4000%.[15]

From the very beginning of his tenure within the C-Suite he took every opportunity to find ways to clean up, if you will, the organizational structure of the organization through careful analysis of the individual processes from the perspective of effectiveness and efficiency.

One tool that came out of this new focus of the organization was the implementation of the GE Workout around 1989. The GE Workout consisted of a very structured system to resolve problems within the organization. The continuous process improvement developed along the paths shown in Figure 2.1.[16]

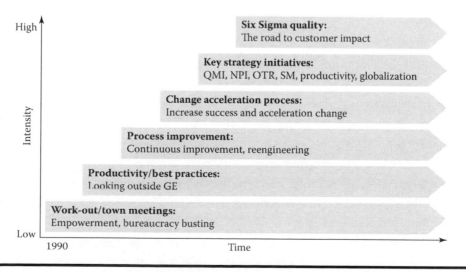

Figure 2.1   Change culture within General Electric.

Welch was firmly against the overbearing bureaucracy found within the GE organization. What he did believe in was the ability of every employee, no matter his or her role within the organization, to have a say in its future. The basic premise of the GE Workout was that cross-functional teams would identify a problem and create solutions to solve that problem. This process of cross-functional teams being the conduit for change within the organization was the impetus for the Workout program.

The GE Workout consisted of a five-step process as I describe next:

Step 1: Problem identification: In the process of delivering the services needed to meet the customer needs, employees determined that there was a problem with the process which prohibited the organization from meeting the customer's deadline. As a result a collaborative effort was made to identify exactly what the process roadblock was and its impact on the organization.

Step 2: Team development: Following the identification of the problem a team was put in place that consisted of both rank and file and management to apply a review process to the indicated problem. The team make-up consisted of both internal and external stakeholders. The key to their inclusion was what the impact was on them from the solution to the problem.

Step 3: Town meeting: Once the solutions to the identified problems were designed the team brought the discussion of the problem to a town meeting, where both the teams and the members of upper management were present. These town meetings could, according to David Ulrich's book on the Workout process, last from 1 to 3 days. Each team presented their findings and recommendations to the management team. The report presentations also included the justification behind the solutions.

Step 4: Upper management decision: At the conclusion of each team presentation, upper management was provided with two alternatives. The first was that they could completely reject the suggestions from the team, but they would have to explain their reasoning for saying no. They were not in a position to just say no or say that they wanted to take it under further consideration.

Step 5: Sponsorship: If upper management gave its approval to go forward with the problem resolution, one of the team members stepped forward[17] as the problem resolution sponsor. It was their responsibility to ensure that the solutions were implemented within 90 days typically.

It involved frequent progress reports back to the organizational management.

If we return to Figure 2.1, we can see that within GE, the workout was the base for the development of change management within the organization. The next step up the ladder was the beginning of the efforts among business organizations to identify the best of the best. In that vein, GE began the process of looking at how similar organizations were handling the same issues. It was the beginning of the Best Practices efforts in American corporations.

Based on the work of Michael Hammer and James Champy, GE began the efforts to reinvent the organization through re-engineering. This effort brought to the forefront the concept of continuous process improvement. The idea was supported to say that in everything we do, there is always a better way to do what we are doing. All levels of the organization were pushed to constantly and consistently review every operation and look for areas where they could produce better results by running more efficiently.

I have already mentioned at several opportunities, and will continue to do so throughout the book, that one of the characteristics of the new cultural model is that it is a never-ending road. As the years passed, a group of GE management began to look at how we could improve the Workout process. Understand it was not that anyone disapproved of the Workout process, it was just this inbred part of the GE culture that you constantly looked at to see how to improve the process to make it more robust. The result was what GE called the CAP.[18]

The CAP pilot was run out of the GE training center at Crotonville, NY, and was originally termed the Leadership Development Series. At the same time Larry Bossidy, who later went on to write the book *Execution*, developed another program with similar elements and goals. The two were combined to form the CAP. It consisted of a model that contained six steps, which were reviewed on the basis of where we are today, where we are going to end up, and how to make the transition. The process began with the requirement of management to lead the change effort. Management had to buy into the change for it to function successfully.

Following management leading the change process, the CAP established the reason why the organization had to share the need across the entire organization. They demonstrated why the change that was introduced needed to cross the entire organization, not departmental silos alone. They demonstrated to the rank and file how this change was going to make their job easier and better. Keep in mind that our ultimate goal is to produce our services or projects cheaper, better, and faster. The rank and file needed to understand what it was that was in the process for them.

Having proven the need for solving the problem, the management turned to creating a vision for the organization. This vision provided a roadmap much as we are doing that established our road to HR excellence.

To this point the organization had established the buy-in by management and convinced the organization at all levels why we needed the change and where we expected to be after the change process. Now it was necessary to get employees away from the feeling that this was nothing more than the fad of the day to a feeling of being in an exciting place and time. This was the time when management got the entire organization behind the efforts to introduce change to the organization.

The final two steps of the model could be considered the most important. First, we needed to ensure that the changes made by the model would last. It does the organization no good to introduce this viable system for change only to have someone say down the road, this is great but I am more comfortable doing things the way we have always done them. One of the methods to ensure longevity of the change process is to measure the progress we have achieved toward our end goal.

We can't have change take place within an organization without one final step. Change means sacrifice. Change means rethinking the way we do things. Each of these means that to achieve our vision of HR excellence we must change both the way the organization is structured and the systems that govern our operations.

Both the GE Workout process and the CAP bring about the required changes in both areas. They teach us how to become better stewards of the organization by locating areas that might be hindering the organization and taking dynamic steps to change the system and the structure. While we improve the systems, we also change the format of the organization through the removal of silo mentality within the organization.

Honeywell

Several years after Allied Signal began their efforts toward process improvement, Honeywell formally put in place their version of the continuous process improvement effort. Renamed the Honeywell Operating system and the Honeywell Quality Value, the two systems were designed around the Six Sigma basics as explained by Motorola and GE.

Honeywell/Allied Signal Merger

In 1999, the management and stakeholders of both firms determined that the best thing for both entities was to merge their two operations. This also required the merger of the four improvement processes into a Lean enterprise and an activity-based management.

Ultimate Improvement Cycle

In 2009, Bob Sproull introduced a new look to the continuous process improvement effort, which combined the three perspectives. This is the same process that I have renamed the TLS Continuum. The partial reason for this combination was a confrontation between those who leaned toward the Lean view of operations, which centered on the removal of wastes, and Six Sigma, that leaned toward establishing the standard of work.

To respond to this conflict, the TLS Continuum looks at the three aspects and develops the model where each step assigns specific responsibilities for the completion of the process. We begin with the Theory of Constraints discussed earlier in this chapter, which now has the goal to identify the obstacles within the system. What is holding up the flow of the process to the customer? Once the obstacle is identified, the L or Lean in the continuum becomes responsible for removing the obstacle.

The final stage of the TLS Continuum, represented by the S, is for Six Sigma. It is here that we establish the standard of work and ensure that all processes are free of any variations.

Notes

1. Eliyahu Goldratt wrote a series of books based on the Theory of Constraints published by the North River Press beginning with *The Goal* and ending with *Isn't It Obvious*. There are five titles in the series.
2. Jeffrey Liker has written a series of books about the TPS, which were mentioned previously.
3. Pande, Peter, et al. *The Six Sigma Way*. New York: McGraw-Hill, 2000.
4. While this is a truly important part of the evolutionary process, there have been many volumes within the marketplace that discuss the TPS in more depth than I. I would refer readers to the work of Jeffrey Liker, who has now written six books on the subject. These books are *The Toyota Way*, *The Toyota Way Fieldbook*, *The Toyota Way to Lean Leadership*, *The Toyota Way to Continuous Improvement*, *Toyota Culture*, and *Toyota Talent*.

5. "Quality Circles." http://enotes.com/quality-circles-reference/quality-circles.
6. http://www.tqe.com/TQM.html.
7. Wikipedia. "W. Edward Deming."
8. http://En.wikepedia.org/W_Edwards_Deming#Key_principles. Can also be found in Mary Walton's *The Deming Management Method*.
9. Liker, Jeffrey. *Toyota Culture*. New York, NY: McGraw-Hill, 2007. P. 111.
10. Taiichi Ohno created the Stand in the Circle concept. It required managers to stand in a circle on the production floor for about 25 minutes and really look at what was going on around them and then to identify the problem and what impact it was having on the organization.
11. Ibid.
12. Lencioni, Patrick. *Silos, Politics and Turf Wars*. San Francisco, CA: Jossey-Bass, 2006.
13. Goldratt, Eliyahu. *The Goal*. Croton-on-the-Hudson: North River Press, 1984. There are actually five titles to the Theory of Constraints tool descriptions.
14. The information herein is based on the material sent to me and conversations I had with Rick Tucci who is the president of Leap Technologies who created the Rapid Workout.
15. http://www.improvefaster.com.
16. For a more in-depth understanding of the GE Workout process, I suggest that readers take a look at David Ulrich's book on the topic. *GE Workout*. New York: McGraw-Hill, 2002.
17. http://en.wikipedia.org/wiki/Jack_Welch.
18. http://www.scribd.com/doc/3240020/GE-WORKOUT-KIT.

Chapter 3

What Is Six Sigma?

In the introduction, I challenged you to consider what direction you were taking your educational career in. My hope is that you chose the direction of becoming a vital partner in the success of your organizations. Assuming you did in fact choose this direction, I indicated that we were beginning a journey of discovery with no real point of an ultimate destination or conclusion.

While the previous chapter looked at the evolution of the total quality movement from Deming to the modern formats, I still did not delineate just what the journey entails. With this chapter and the next one, I begin to lay out the characteristics of that journey.

I facilitate a 14-hour training program titled Achieving HR Excellence through Six Sigma in which the opening exercise asks the participants to think about what they would tell the chief executive officer (CEO) if they were asked to explain just what this thing is that we call Six Sigma.

As educational professionals I would ask you the same question: what would you tell the school administration Six Sigma is?

I would guess that if you asked a random selection of individuals both within and outside the educational community what Six Sigma is you would receive a wide variety of responses. I can tell you from personal experience that when I say I have a Six Sigma Black Belt, a fair number think I am talking about some martial arts discipline. From the business perspective their responses can be narrowed down into three responses. Before we delve into just what the Six Sigma methodology is, we need to consider these responses more in depth.

It Is a Manufacturing Thing

In the beginning of the total quality movement, as I discussed in Chapter 2, the world was firmly entrenched within the industrial age following World War II. An organization's brand and reputation in the marketplace was based on the quality of the products they produced. Deming and those that followed him were reviewing problems that arose out of the resulting process. The constant goal was to produce end-user products that were readily available to the marketplace and that the end users would pay for. The end user is seeking products that are delivered and that perform the usage for which they were intended. They are seeking products that are free from defects making them less valuable to their organization.

Deming, Ishikawa, and Smith saw processes that were basically flawed from the very nature of their existence. These processes were not meeting the needs of their customers due to reworks because of defects in the production process.

As continuous process improvement students we will concede that the vast majority of the Six Sigma training programs in existence are the result of manufacturing issues. Organizations are looking at the widgets we produce and trying to determine why we are not meeting the customer needs. Some of the solutions are very simple; some are more complex in nature.

In the manufacturing space, we are able to see, identify, and find solutions to these problems. We have a physical object, which either met the voice of the customer, or it did not. The rank-and-file employee could, by the very nature of his or her job responsibilities, know if the process was not working. In many cases these problems arose out of a backlog of material coming down the assembly line and no place to put it. Every member of the organization could somewhat easily comprehend this scenario.

But what happens when the organizational structure has similar problems? What happens when we are in a position where we can't see, identify, or feel the end widget? We, on the transactional side of the equation, are in that position.

Like the production side of the coin, the transactional side also produces widgets. The difference is that our widgets are less tangible in nature. Our widgets, as Ken Miller argues in his book *We Don't Make Widgets*,[1] are the process outputs that are generated as schools deliver their services to serve the stakeholders of the organization. Just as in the production realm, our processes have critical outputs that can affect the entire organization. These critical outputs are what we use to align education with the school strategic initiatives. Our widgets are items like the curriculum, the skills developed in our students, policy descriptions when we create handbooks and manuals, the end results of investigations into campus issues such as bullying and harassment and other final reports. However, these widgets are still a vital part of the educational organization. Because they are not tangible in nature, our widgets are not something that a staff person can necessarily turn to and say wait a minute, something is wrong. While the widgets are not measureable like on the factory floor, the educational function is a factory of sorts. This means that the output from the educational factory is measureable just like if we were on that factory floor. Our educational widgets are still able to produce credible, verifiable data measure points to solve the process defects.

We Tried That and It Didn't Work in Our Organization

As human beings we have a tendency to want the newest and greatest tool that becomes available to make our lives "easier." Business annuals are filled with examples of management decisions to get that latest great tool. What are also prevalent are incidents where management tried to take short cuts to implement these tools, only to be met with disaster.

The implementation of Six Sigma in an organization requires some fundamental changes to the organization. When we try and implement the latest tool without thinking it through, the premise going in is flawed. Six Sigma-related improvement efforts fail because the organization has not made the required changes to the basis for making decisions. The perspective on the educational marketplace needs to shift from the organization to focus on what the customer wants and needs. In many cases, as I will show later in this book, when we introduce Six Sigma to an organization, the first requirement is a culture change. Administration touts the change but wants to do it on the terms of the organization at that moment or in the past. It is these kinds of circumstances that bring about the response that the system does not work. These are the kinds of circumstances that bring out the response that it is not right for our organization. While the administration wants the successes that have been reported, they are not interested in making the changes we will discuss in future chapters. The Six Sigma process is a structured response to a problem, but one of the critical factors here is that to fully realize the benefits to the schools and the customers, we need to create a new way of doing business. Failure to achieve this organizational change is what leads to the failure of Six Sigma improvement efforts.

It Is Too Highly Complex to Be Used in Most Organizations

As I discussed in the last chapter, the whole basis of the total quality movement was the work of Dr. Deming, who was by trade a statistician. His fellow champions of the quality movement were mostly engineers. By their very nature they are steeped in detailed analysis of data. I totally understand that high math is not everyone's cup of tea. Further, this high demand for high-level math has lost followers on the way along our journey. Motorola today no longer offers the high-level training it used to due to the complexity of the data and the training requirements.

It is my belief that this is a nonissue. If we have the data and the right software we can resolve this issue. Jay Arthur, of KnowledgeWare, in his book *Free, Perfect and Now,*[2] suggests that with the right information, you as transactional managers only need to utilize seven tools out of the toolbox we will discuss later in this book.

Despite the reactions to the responses shown here, in almost every case they have failed to recognize that there is sufficient evidentiary data to show that the Six Sigma methodology is, when used with administrative total support, a highly effective tool to improve your schools. The Six Sigma methodology shows your schools how to improve your performance issues in clear and precise steps. The steps are appropriate on the plant floor as well as in the classroom or the school administration.

To fully explain what Six Sigma is, I am going to backtrack just for a moment on my previous statement. To truly understand the basis for the Six Sigma processes we do need to look at its statistical side more in depth.

Remember your school days when we pushed instructors to grade on a curve. The intent was to identify where the average score landed and to grade the exceptions on a curve. This curve was manifested in a tool called the bell curve as shown in Figure 3.1.[3]

Our argument to the professor was that based on the fact that the scores on the examination fell outside the expected grade ranges, we wanted them to grade the exam based on the results of the curve which hopefully would result in higher grades for all after the scores were reviewed. As human beings, as we have discussed earlier, we push for that nirvana we call perfection. Our ultimate goal in life and within the school is to reach a point where our output is considered to be as free from defects or as close to perfection as possible. The bell curve provides us

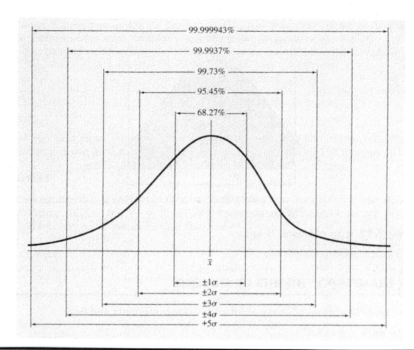

Figure 3.1   The bell curve.

with the ability to view our data and determine how close we have come to reaching that goal.

If you remember our discussion of the history of the total quality movement and the role of Motorola, I discussed that one of the goals of Bill Smith was to find a way to count defects within their processes.

Coming from the Greek, *sigma* refers to the summation of the numbers or quantities indicated.[4] In statistical terms, the term *sigma* allows us to measure the data in the bell curve and the rate of the variation within our processes. It represents the amount of variation that occurs relative to the specific customer's specifications. The bell curve tells us that in most cases, we allow for one standard deviation above or below the mean score. Each deviation from the mean is equivalent to 34%, above and below the average point or the point of error-free processes. The bell curve provides us with a clear perspective on how close we are coming to meet the voice of the customer. We can take the bell curve and apply it to a defects per million opportunities (DPMO) chart.

If we review the table in Figure 3.2, we find that as our DPMO decrease, the level of the yield or those items that meet the required customer specifications increases. The smaller the variation from the

YIELD	DPMO	SIGMA
99.9999	1	6.27
99.9997	3	6.04
99.9990	10	5.77
99.99	100	5.22
99.90	1000	4.59
99.00	10000	3.83
98.00	20000	3.55
97.00	30000	3.38
96.00	40000	3.25
95.00	50000	3.14
94.00	60000	3.05

Figure 3.2   Sigma value chart. The table assumes a 1.5 sigma shift because processes tend to exhibit instability of that magnitude over time. In other words, although statistical tables indicate that 3.4 defects/million is achieved when 4.5 process standard deviations (sigma) are between the mean and the closest specification limit, the target is raised to 6.0 standard deviations to accommodate adverse process shifts over time and still produce only 3.4 defects per million opportunities.

requirement the closer we get to the goal of perfection. As a result, when we reach a level of Six Sigma, the defect rate or the variation from the voice of customer is so small that the resulting product or service is 99.99966% on target to the customer specifications. It is hard to get much closer to our goal of perfection than that. We usually display these results in what is referred to as a Six Sigma defects per million opportunities chart as shown in Figure 3.2.[5]

Toyota through their Toyota Production System have shown that at its very essence, the Six Sigma methodology is a unique, structured system to resolve workplace critical issues. Some organizations have tried to approach the process from the point of view of an established quality department. Six Sigma can't operate as a silo and expect to achieve the goals we anticipate from our continuous process improvement efforts. Its goal is to take the culture of process improvement and imbed it in cross-functional personnel determining where the problems are and potential solutions to the issues that arise. These potential solutions are not a finance problem, nor a Human Resources problem—they are an organizational problem. It is not necessarily squarely centered on the ultimate results but rather on how we got there. The structured system is designed to show us how to utilize the toolbox that will be discussed in the next chapter to resolve problems through the creation of creditable data that shows us why a particular process is not working the way the organization was expecting.

Six Sigma Roles

While I have stressed several times that the key to making Six Sigma work is the functioning of cross-functional teams, the process has its own team responsibilities. This is not to say that I am talking about command and control here, but rather who has the responsibilities to guide the ship and make sure that the team is staying on task. This section will look at each of the roles, the training required, and what their contribution is to the finished product.

Senior Administrator

The senior administrator role in the process is to gain stakeholder buy-in to the change process. They are the ones who make the pitch to the administration and the school boards on what the problem is, why we need to solve the problem, and why the proposed project is the correct route to take. They are also responsible for conducting reviews of project progress and reporting the results of the review both to the cross-functional teams and to the stakeholders of the organization.

Executive Committee

Comprised of the members of senior administration, the executive committee pushes the methodology out into the educational organization. While there is some degree of discussion about the role of senior management in the process, if the executive committee and thus the senior management do not buy into the process it will not result in successful conclusions. They also have the responsibility to ensure that the required resources needed by the project team are made available.

While it would be helpful, there is no published requirement that either the senior administrator or the members of the executive team must have any in-depth training into the methodology and how it works.

Champion (Project)

The role of the champion is to be the rudder of the project. They are the ones who make sure the teams stay on target and are working to delivering the milestones when they say they will be delivered. They are responsible for reviewing the project's long-term impact on the educational institution. If the team runs into an obstacle, it is the champion who helps them get around a solution. The champion in addition holds the purse strings for the project, authorizing the release of fund for various aspects of the project. Because of the nature of the duties of the project champion, the person in this role should have earned at least a yellow belt so they have some understanding of the process the team is working through.

Process Owner

Since the first word in this book, I have made mention that the critical factor in the success of the Six Sigma methodology is the voice of the customer. The project owner is that voice. They are the ones who have direct impact on the project. In today's business climate, many managers and employees ask the question "what is in it for me?" The process owner is no different. They know they have a problem and have asked the cross-functional team to assist in finding a solution. The expectation is that the process owner is going to be able to find the positive solution to the problem because of the process we have undertaken, and thus we will have met the voice of the customer.

From this point on, the roles begin to require more in-depth training in how the process works. There are many sources out there to obtain the training both live and online, and I will not suggest to the reader what is the best direction from which to obtain the training. I did, however, need a standard source to describe the basic training requirements going forward so I turned to the certification section of the American Society for Quality[6] (ASQ) website as a basis for the resources in this area.

I need to divert our attention for a moment to an issue within the quality industry at present. There is much discussion underway about whether we have, since the idea's inception at Motorola, trained too many "belts" within our organizations. If you poll professionals within the quality field you will receive a mix of responses. Steven Bonacorsi, president of the International Standard for Lean Six Sigma (ISLSS), suggests that there is a philosophy called the Corporate DNA of Deployment, based on substantial, creditable, and verifiable data that has determined that there is a basic formula as to how many belts are needed for our efforts to become sustainable, self-sustained deployment through the organization. ISLSS suggests that you should have one Master Black Belt for every 15–25 Black Belts, 0.05%–1% Black Belts, and 4%–6% Green Belts within your organization. Motorola had the formula that you needed 1 Master Black Belt for every 10 Black Belts and 1 Black Belt for every 10 Green Belts. General Electric went so far as to require any 1 seeking leadership positions within the organization to have at least their green belt. The real question is, have we concentrated too much on the certification process and not enough on the system for resolving the organizational problems?

Master Black Belt

A Master Black Belt is expected to have a minimum of 5 years of experience or to have successfully completed 10 Six Sigma Black Belt projects showing expertise in three areas: teaching, coaching, and mentoring; occupational experience and responsibility; and technical knowledge and innovation of the field. It is inherent that they have clear knowledge of strategic plan development and deployment, cross-functional competencies, and mentoring responsibilities.

The Master Black Belt is the leader of the Six Sigma improvement process and in some cases also will take on the responsibilities of the project champion in smaller organizations. They are also responsible for the implementation of programs that will aid the continuous improvement effort along with training the Black Belts and Green Belts in the Six Sigma methodology.

The corporate DNA of deployment suggests that there should be one Master Black Belt for each 15 to 25 Black Belts within the organization.

Black Belt

The next level down in the pyramid is that of the Black Belts. Black Belts are expected to have completed two projects with a signed affidavit on each, plus 3 years of work experience. To be successful they must be able to explain the philosophy and principles to others within the organization. It is also preferred that they have at least a 4-year college degree. They become the first line supervisor of the process. The immediate supervisor is the Master Black Belt. It is the expectation of the organization that a Black Belt will complete between four and six projects per year which will result in $250,000 to $500,000 in savings for the organization. Both the Master Black Belt and the Black Belts are full-time in their responsibilities, so their primary vision is on how to improve the organization from the perspective of removing waste and variation from the processes.

Green Belt

The Green Belt, like the Black Belt, should have at least 3 years of experience in quality efforts so that they can be familiar with the tools. Under guidelines from ASQ, the candidate for a Green Belt will have completed 64 hours of instruction in a classroom situation learning the methodology. In the course of their duties they will analyze and solve elementary quality problems. They may also lead smaller teams. In most organizations the role of a Green Belt is a part-time one in nature. The projects they work on are in the range of $25,000–$50,000 in potential savings for the organization. Their improvement efforts pay for the program training.

Yellow Belt

The Yellow Belt certification is reserved for those individuals who will be assigned as team members on the improvement efforts. It typically requires between 14 and 20 hours of training in the tools of the Six Sigma methodology. While Yellow Belts will not be leading specific projects, it is necessary that they understand when and how they should use the individual tools at each stage of the process. They also learn how to relate these concepts to the business's overall strategy. Remember that the ultimate results of the project process are the creation of creditable, verifiable data so they need to understand how to read the data points so they can be interpreted correctly.

White Belt

The bottom layer of the roles within our process improvement efforts is the White Belts. This could be opened to anyone within the organization who wants a general knowledge of the process. Typically, a White Belt candidate undergoes only about 8 hours of training that is centered on an overview of the process and the tools.

Six Sigma Methodology Themes[7]

The purpose of this chapter has not been to provide the reader with a full discussion of Six Sigma. There are others who have come before me who can do a way better job of that, such as Michael George and Peter Pande. My purpose was to give you a very brief overview of what this tool is all about. We will in the next chapter get more in depth regarding the toolbox and how it is utilized. In summary of this point there are two areas that we must consider. The first is a review of the basics of the methodology, and the second is to look at when it is most appropriate to consider implementing the toolbox. As I discussed, there are some very basic tenets to the concept. These tenets need to be in place in order for any continuous process improvement effort to be successful.

First is that there must be a *genuine focus on the customer.* The customer is the driver for the success of our organizations. Many organizations make strategic decisions based on what they think the customer wants or needs. The real key is to make a concerted effort to get inside the head of your customers (both internal and external) to determine exactly what they need and are willing to pay for. As we will see later in this book, there are some types of waste that affect every organization. These waste situations arise when we are not focused on the customer.

The second tenet is that the process is *data and fact driven management.* It is critical to the success of the process improvement effort that the needs of the customer are based on data and facts that are verifiable, meaning that there is proof of the results that we are reporting. In addition, the data and facts must be creditable in nature. There must be some basis for the information we have generated.

The third tenet is that it is *process focused management and improvement.* The problem-solving structure presented by Six Sigma is focused on solving the problem at hand. The resulting workout projects are focused on that goal. We have a process in hand to identify, correct, and maintain the improvements we make to our organizations.

The fourth tenet is *proactive management.* Many organizations operate on the tendency to try and solve a problem after it becomes an issue. This leads to an environment where we are constantly trying to play catch-up. Six Sigma pushes us to actually look for areas where the internal processes are not meeting that customer focus. It calls for the organization to confront the problems before they become a critical issue.

The fifth tenet is the existence of *boundaryless collaboration.* The goal of this effort is to have the total organization in alignment with the organizational strategic initiatives and objectives. This is not something that can be done by just the administration or Human Resources or department heads or Finance. It will only be successful if we have total buy-in across the entire organization. It is for this reason that each improvement project is based on the intellectual input from every end of the organization. The views of the frontline human capital assets are just as important as, if not more important than, the management of the organization. The effort will be only as successful as the organization's ability to remove the functional silos that are so characteristic of many of our organizations.

The final tenet is that of centering our efforts on *driving for perfection and tolerating failure*. I stated at the beginning of this chapter that it is a natural human tendency for us to strive to be perfect. This drive occurs both in the business world and in our personal piece of the world. It is based on the realization that while we are striving to be perfect we will, in no way, be right every time.

With the understanding of the nature of the Six Sigma process and its role within our organizations, the last item to consider before we begin our look at the methodology in earnest is to answer the question as to when we use this tool within our organizational structure. The best suggestions come from the work of Mikel Harry and Richard Schroeder, who in their book *Six Sigma: The Breakthrough Management Strategy Revolutionizing the World's Top Corporations*[8] suggested that there are five indicators that provide us with the basis for entering into a continuous process improvement effort.

- *We don't know, what we don't know*: The reason why many process obstacles are in existence is because they are in plain sight but are overlooked. They are overlooked because in the stream of things we are used to operating in the path we have always conducted business. For example, I recently facilitated a seminar in which one of the teams working through a process map of their recruiting function discovered that in the course of recruiting new talent for the organization, the job requisition was reviewed three times—by the same person. When asked why, the response was "we don't know." These obstacles or constraints remain hidden until typically a customer is ready to take their business elsewhere.

- *We can't act on what we don't know*: A customer is having a problem with our meeting their needs, and what have they done—they have stewed on the issue. While we want to strive to provide perfect customer service, we can't do that if we do not know there is a problem. As a supplement to the first indicator, if we are not aware of the problem, or we have not looked for the defects or waste in our processes on a continuous basis, then we can't act to solve the problem.

- *We won't know until we search*: Your customer calls and says we are having a horrible time meeting our needs with the way your school is delivering the end widget. Do you know, from the conversation, what the cause is? I suspect that you do not. The Six Sigma methodology, as we will see in Chapter 4, provides us with the vehicles to find that cause.

■ *We won't search until we question*: We totally understand that everyone hates change. There is a wide variety of resources in the market that tells why this exists. This is not the place to discuss that field of thought. The point where we are going is that in most cases, the causes of these non-value-added parts of our processes are there within your organization if you only took the time to look for them. As we will see in the next chapter, there are always possibilities to improve our processes; we just have to take the time to question why we do what we do.

■ *We don't question what we don't measure*: Begin with an assumption of a fact of the business world. Everything we do within the organization is based on a step-by-step process. If we do this, we get this. If we do that, we get this. Each and every step produces data. If we produce data we can measure it. As we will see in the next chapter, the measurement stage of the process is critical to our success in the efforts to meet the voice of the customer.

Notes

1. Miller, Ken. *We Don't Make Widgets*. Washington, DC: Governing Books, 2010.
2. Arthur, Jay. *Free, Perfect and Now*. Denver, CO: KnowledgeWare, 2012. PP. 37–40.
3. From the St. Petersburg College Black Belt Training Program.
4. Dictionary.com. http://dictionary.reference.com/browse/sigma?s=t.
5. Part of the materials from the St Petersburg College Six Sigma Black Belt Training Program.
6. Information on the certification process and individual belt responsibilities can be found on the ASQ website at http://www.asq.org/certification/control/right-for-you.
7. Taken from the material presented as part of the Six Sigma training at St Petersburg College.
8. Mikel, Harry, and Richard Schroeder. *Six Sigma: The Breakthrough Management Strategy Revolutionizing the World's Top Corporations*. New York: Crown Publishing, 2005.

Chapter 4

Six Sigma Toolbox

As I explained in Chapter 1, we have undertaken a journey to transform our schools into a new business model centered on the business strategic initiatives of the educational institution. In Chapter 3, I gave you a brief overview of what this methodology we call Six Sigma is. Our primary point was that it was a proven methodology. In the previous chapter, I discussed what Six Sigma is and why it is important to your school. One of these points was that the Six Sigma methodology is a proven, accurate tool for guiding an organization through the process of resolving issues. However, the process only works when you have a set of tools to get you there. Like I did with the bell curve in Chapter 3, I can provide you with a model for that process.

Take yourself back in time to your high school science classes. I am willing to bet (and I am not a betting person) that every one of your science classes began with a discussion of the scientific method. If you don't remember precisely don't fret, just know that it was done. I taught science for 6 years, and I started out every class with this very discussion. The scientific method was designed to provide us with a standard method of solving experiments that took place within the lab. It consisted of a sequential series of steps that took you through the experiment (Figure 4.1).

The scientific method is based on creditable, verifiable facts and data, which are developed as you walk through the experiment before you. The first step is that you *formulate a question*. The question asks us to consider several factors. What is the problem that the experiment is considering? Almost as important is why are we facing the problem? It asks us to consider what may have occurred before this point and what the after effects on our natural system are.

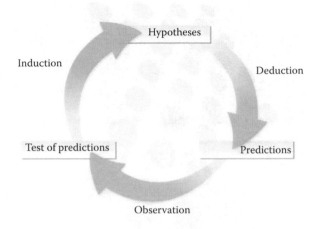

Figure 4.1   Scientific method. (From http://www.experiment-resources.com/what-is-the-scientific-method.html.)

Following the development of a hypothesis, the second step within the scientific method is *the prediction* of what is necessary to verify that our hypothesis is correct. It looks for concrete evidence to prove that what we think is going on is actually taking place. Having completed our anticipation of what the solution is we can move on to the next step.

The third step is *testing* our prediction to see if what we believe is going on is actually happening. It seeks to find the most correct response to our experimental data to determine the best course to follow to solve our problem as we explained in the hypothesis.

The fourth step in the process is to *analyze* our results from the testing and compare it to the results we have seen. The objective is to provide creditable, verifiable data, which either proves or disproves our expected solution to the problem. If the facts don't support our hypothesis, we go back and retry the solution further or explore other options.

The final or fifth step is *conclusions*. You are asked to review your results, the test performed, the results of your analysis, and report whether you solved the experiment in a verifiable manner.

Wikipedia[1] tells us that what sets this method apart from other tools is that scientists seek to let the real world speak for the results, supporting the theory behind an experiment with creditable, verifiable evidence that provides us with the correct solutions. It also requires that the steps taken to solve the hypothesis question must be repeatable, so that others looking at the same problem can follow the same track of inquiry.

Scientific method	DMAIC process
Construct a hypothesis	Define the problem
Test your hypothesis	Measure the problem
Analyze your data	Analyze the results
Draw a conclusion	Improve the process
Communicate results	Control the process

Figure 4.2 Comparisons between scientific method and DMAIC process.

The Six Sigma methodology has its own scientific method; we call it the DMAIC (define-measure-analyze-improve-control) process. In this chapter, we will take a look at each stage of the process in depth. At the same time, we will look at both the business cases and the tools that are appropriate to each stage. The stages in this process are *define, measure, analyze, improve, and control.* Before we begin the next stage of our journey, can you match these stages to the scientific method you used in the science classroom back in high school (Figure 4.2)?

Define Stage

In Chapter 3, I made reference to the work of Dr. Mikel Harry[2] who in his book discussed when Six Sigma and it methodology should be implemented. One of those factors was *we don't know what we don't know.* The *define* stage is where we begin to identify what it is we don't know. It is where we create what we think the solution is to the problem.

The *define* stage begins with a review of the process and what the customer is telling us is not being delivered to them. Frequently, the input at this point is from within the organization. The organization looks at the problem from the inside looking out, rather than from the point of view of what the customer is telling us. Having determined what we think is wrong, we also determine what we would expect the process to look like once the process is completed.

Once we have determined the business case for the problem, we can begin the process of implementing the project. The initial step is to get upper management buy-in for the DMAIC within the organization. In order to achieve this goal, we must demonstrate to them that there is a long-lasting benefit to the organization. One of the tools we use to achieve this is the project charter.

The project charter (a copy of the charter can be found on the following pages) is a concise form that lays out the project scope and work. It begins with identifying the project that you are planning on working on. It answers the question regarding what you expect to achieve. It also identifies which organization or department is sponsoring the project. This is typically the one that will gain the most contribution from the process improvement efforts. If you remember, in the last chapter we also discussed the role of the various human capital assets involved in Six Sigma projects. One of those roles was that of the project sponsor. The sponsor is the key to the success of the project as they are putting their name on the project as being one of utmost importance. They are the gatekeeper to keep the project active through management upper levels.

There is no chance of success in an improvement project if you remain enclosed within your functional cocoon. The key is to look at the problem from all angles within the organization. The team of individuals who are responsible for implementation must come from a cross section of the entire organization, and include a representative from every segment that is touched by the problem in question. The next part of the charter form shows the names of the cross-functional team members and what their specific roles are within the project. Some, like the finance representative, may be obvious, but other team members will have vital roles to play even though their role might be less obvious. Still, you want to designate their exact role within the project team for each member.

The ultimate goal from the project is to meet the needs as expressed by the customer. In order to complete the project in detail we need to identify who are the stakeholders who are most likely to gain the most from a successful outcome and further, to identify what the benefit is. The next block on the charter requires the project sponsor to sign off and date the form. It is from here that we begin to develop the inner factors in the project.

The cross-functional team prepares a process map, if you will, of the project. It establishes a timeline using a Gantt chart.[3] One of the outcomes of the project schedule is to develop a set of milestones which are recorded on the project charter. A milestone becomes an indicator as to how the project is advancing.

When I underwent my training for the Black Belt, my project was dealing with the effectiveness of training an organization's human capital assets. In the project charter, I listed seven milestones. Each milestone indicated a target date for delivery, the actual date for delivery, and sponsor approvals. The milestones that were indicated in my project charter were:

Determine the scope of the project
Prepare and submit the project charter
Determine the evaluation methods
Analyze the training data
Construct the dashboards
Construct the balance scorecard
Deliver the final product to the stakeholders

Following the milestones, the next task is to develop a detailed description of the problem that you believe is present within your organization. It may also be an opportunity statement if you are introducing a new process.

Project Charter Statement

Project name / title:				
Sponsoring organization:				
Project sponsor:				

Team members (Name)	Role

Principal stakeholder	Proposed benefit

Sponsor approval signature / date:

Preliminary plan (Milestones)		Target date	Actual date	Approvals

Project name / title:
Problem / opportunity statement
Project goal: solution / recommendation
Resources requested (what you need, $, personnel, time, etc.)
Project impact statement

Having established the problem statement, the cross-functional team now develops, for management review, the goal of the project. This includes your proposed solution and recommendations for changes within the organization. It is at this point that you may begin to see some pushback from within the organization from those aspects that are reluctant or afraid of changing what they have done for time eternal.

You not only want but need buy-in from upper management for the process to work successfully, so one of the data points that must be presented is what is the process going to cost the organization. This section of the charter asks the team to delineate the resources needed. For each resource requested, you need to tell management precisely what you need in terms of funds, time away from traditional work expectations, and added equipment. The list could go on forever, but it needs to be detailed to provide a clear picture of what it will take to achieve your goal.

Regardless of whether you are a teacher or the superintendent of the school, your immediate question is WIFM or What's In it For Me? The final section of the project charter is space for the team to delineate what the impact on the school will be if you are successful in completing the project. The project impact should also provide a view of the dollar savings that could be expected if the changes you are suggesting come to be within the organization.

The Six Sigma methodology is comprised of more than one tool from which you can choose to assist in your project. We usually define the tools from two perspectives. The first is from the Lean side. These tools tend to be less costly and quicker to introduce than the full Six Sigma side. Figure 4.3 shows a chart with the tools within the methodology. We will repeat the chart in each of the phases with the precise tools at that stage highlighted in bold text.

I totally understand that if you were on the factory floor some of these tools would be more beneficial than within the educational space. But there are specific tools that can benefit your processes. The first tool from the Lean side

DMAIC step	Six Sigma tools	Lean tools
Define	**Voice of customer** **Project charter** **Project critical to quality definition** **High-level process map**	**Value definition**
Measure	Quality function deployment Measurement system analysis	Value stream mapping
Analyze	Process capability analysis FMEA Benchmarking Hypothesis testing Graphical tools	Line balance Takt time calculation
Improve	Regression analysis Design of experiments Risk assessment	5 S Establish flow/pull system SCORE events
Control	Determine new process capability Statistical process control Control plants	Poka Yoke Visual management

Figure 4.3　Six Sigma methodology tool box: Define stage.

is that of value definition. We cannot begin to understand what the customer wants and needs until we understand what constitutes "value" to them. As a result, one of the critical tools is for the team to construct a working definition of the term value. It needs to be based on what the customer tells you what is important from your organization. Part of the process is to survey the customers to ask them what is important. This definition cannot be based on what you think is of value to them. The voice of the customer is based on three specific components. The customer is asked to look at the features of the product or service from the perspective of faster, better, and cheaper. By *faster* we mean that the widget is delivered with activities that truly meet the customer's needs. Based on those needs, your organization has removed any steps in the process that add time to the delivery. By *better* we mean that the product or service is free from defects. We do not serve the client's needs when we deliver incomplete or faulty services to them. The final perspective is that of *cheaper*. In this arena, we look to deliver the service as inexpensively as possible.

Another tool that is valuable at this point is a high-level process map. Remember we mentioned at the beginning of this chapter that one of the utilization indicators is that we don't know what we don't know. The high-level process map becomes the initial look at what we don't know. Following in exact order, with simple blocks and arrows, the entire process is laid out for a view of how we are delivering the service we have been requested. From our 2-day course we can tell you that when a process map is created, some really amazing things have come to light.

Once the process map is complete, the two remaining tools of advantage to educational professionals are the Ishikawa Fishbone Diagram and the SIPOC analysis. The fishbone diagram was created to look at six elements of any process. It looks at management and its role in any decision. Depending on their attitude toward change, management can make or break the effort. The second element is the people involved. We explained the process we are undertaking to the line employee, but do they understand what's in it for them if we do make the necessary change or if we don't? The third element is the method we use to resolve the problems within the organization. We know we have a problem, but how do we resolve those problems. Is there a structured way that you resolve the issues, or is each problem resolved in an ad hoc manner? The fourth element is measurement. We have, through the process, accumulated some data but what do we do with those data points? The fifth element is that of machines. In looking at your process map, have you attempted to automate parts of the process? What equipment is required to complete the project charter milestones?

The sixth and final element is the materials used by the process. This could range from the textbooks to the forms that administration uses to administer the policies and procedures of the organization.

For each of the elements, the team asks the organization what are the results if we, for example, have a management philosophy that runs counter to our expressed goals? What does that do to the total integrity of the process we are trying to implement?

The final tool of the *define stage* is the SIPOC analysis. Taking our process map we begin to look at the total process. From there, we identify who our suppliers are? We are administering processes that are involved with the acquisition of talent for the organization. What sources are we using to achieve that point? This would include suppliers both within and outside of the organization. The next step is to ask yourself, if we use supplier A, as an example, what is it they contribute to the process. Having identified what they provide, to which process is the input assigned? The assumption is that once we identify those steps then what is the ultimate output and who is it delivered to? Let's look at a simple example.

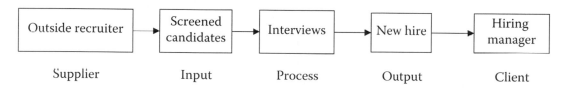

Outside recruiter	Screened candidates	Interviews	New hire	Hiring manager
Supplier	Input	Process	Output	Client

With the conclusion of the steps in the *define stage*, we move to the next step within the improvement scientific method—the *measure stage*.

Measure Stage

In the second step of the scientific method, we are taught that once we have established our hypothesis regarding what we believe the solution is to the problem, we then turn our sights on the testing of that hypothesis. This is achieved by conducting a series of experiments to determine whether the results confirm or disprove the hypothesis. It is standard work within the scientific community. The *measure stage* of the Six Sigma methodology is no different.

During this stage of the DMAIC methodology, we begin to look at what the process is telling us. In Chapter 3, I discussed the utilization indicators that were put forward by Dr. Harry in which one of the points discussed was that *we don't question what we don't measure.*

The intent of the *measure stage* is to review our processes from the VOC perspective to see if the process is, in fact, meeting those demands. The business case for the *measure stage* asks us to explore six specific questions regarding our current processes. Each of the following questions asks us to question why we are doing things the way we have been doing them. This is not to say that every time you measure the process you will find something that is out of variance from the needs of the client but if we don't question the process we will not know.

Question 1: How Do We Measure the VOC Issues?

The organization is confronted with operating results that indicate that somewhere within the organization something is directly affecting the end results. Upper management understands there is a problem but is unclear about the cause. The project charter and the project team have identified what they believe is the source of the obstacle. The project charter has laid out our hypothesis. We all understand that there is an issue. The real question is how do we determine what the nature of the problem is? How do we reliably arrive at data points that verify the outcomes of the processes? As a result, we need to go back to the project charter and test what we believe is the problem. Whether you are in the classroom or in the front office, every day we are confronted with processes that govern how productive the organization is within the marketplace. It is within those processes that certain steps are causing these problems.

In the scientific method step we test the hypothesis. The foremost way we test the hypothesis is to create an experiment that will either prove or disprove our concept developed in the testing of the hypothesis. It is important to recognize that as we conduct these experiments we are creating data points, which aid us in determining the outcome of the testing process. Recognize that these data points have only two results. On the one hand they tell us that the data proves our hypothesis and we can proceed with the rest of the process or it tells us that we were wrong in what we expected, and then we have to return to the experiment stage and further test or change the hypothesis.

Every process, whether it is in the classroom or in the administrative offices, contains key performance indicators (KPIs) which tell your organization whether you are meeting the needs of your customers. One of the first steps is to identify the indicators and how we are going to measure them. I am not concerned about whether you are following the works of individuals in this field such as Dr. Jac Fitz-Enz or Dr. Wayne Casio, we need to establish the metrics you will use to determine the solutions. These metrics must clearly state exactly what we are measuring and why they are of particular concern to the process in question.

Question 2: What Is the Source for the Process Data?

As we determined in the previous question, we need to establish the metrics and KPIs for our processes to determine whether we have an obstacle to the workflow or not. Having the KPIs and the metrics is one thing, but the other side of the equation is where does the data come from? Is the data only based on the internal results? Is the data only based on the customer's view of the process? Does the data include the input from the suppliers to the process?

Among the most common metrics used within the educational arena are the number of students who graduate and the percentage of students with sufficient skills to complete the subject matter. Where do you get your data from to determine the metric? In regards to the number of students who graduate, it typically is defined as the total number of graduates or the total number who graduate in the normal 12 years. But the source of the metric data can vary. Do we start from the point of enrolment in Kindergarten or do we begin when they enter high school? The key is knowing where the data is located and what the source of the metric data points is.

Question 3: Does the Data Tell Us the Real Current State?

In a series of breakout/meeting presentations that is offered to the clients of Daniel Bloom & Associates, Inc., we ask those in attendance a simple question. You are sitting at your desk and the financial statements for your department arrive on your desk. What do you do with them? The vast majority of those that have responded answer that they basically check to ensure that there are no errors in calculations. That is fine, but those numbers may also carry another story behind them. Consider that in your process the client requires delivery in 3 days for an important deadline. Due to your internal processes you deliver it in 7 days. There are costs involved in the missed deadlines. They may be external costs or they may be in the service level agreement which says if the client needs the output in 3 days and you deliver in 7 the organization may incur a penalty for being late. We need to challenge the numbers in order to see if the process is behaving the way we expect it to. When we review the financials as in our previous example we need to do so with an eye toward looking at the process and seeing if the picture we have is in reality what is actually happening.

Question 4: What Does the Existing Process Tell Us?

Part of the measurement process is to gain a picture of what the current process is doing. Consider, for example, this scenario from a real-life client. They were making a product and from every indication they were completing the processes on time but the client was complaining of late delivery. The process metrics showed no real reason for this. When they looked further they found that the process was completed on schedule, but the finished products sat on the loading dock for 7 additional days causing late delivery. The production process was telling the organization that they were following the service level agreement, but external factors were making the process unreliable.

Question 5: How Does the Current Process Operate?

The flip side of the coin is when the quality review of the product or service shows that there are some defects in the processes. The question then becomes why the process is showing the problems. When you look, for example, at your recruitment process, why does the process appear to show problems? In a recent seminar we had a team reviewing their recruitment process to see why it tended to drag at times. It appears that in the course of hiring a new team member, the job requisition was reviewed three times—by the same person. The result was that the process dragged because of the required time for the manager to review a document that they had already reviewed.

Question 6: How Does the Current State of the Process Match the VOC?

The final question is really at the heart of all of our processes. From an internal view, we know what our processes tell the organization. Remember, however, that the true basis of the success of the organization is how close our processes meet the VOC. With this in mind, does the process output tell you the same thing that it tells your customer? The customer, whether internal or external, is the critical part of the chain and so the real indicator of the success of the process or failure comes from the perspective of how the customer views it. Part of the *measure stage* is to measure the process from

DMAIC step	Six Sigma tools	Lean tools
Define	Voice of customer Project charter Project critical to quality definition High-level process map	Value definition
Measure	**Quality function deployment** **Measurement system analysis**	**Value stream mapping**
Analyze	Process capability analysis FMEA Benchmarking Hypothesis testing Graphical tools	Line balance Takt time calculation
Improve	Regression analysis Design of experiments Risk assessment	5 S Establish flow/pull system SCORE events
Control	Determine new process capability Statistical process control Control plants	Poka Yoke Visual management

Figure 4.4 Six sigma methodology tool box: Measure stage.

the client as the end user (Figure 4.4). Is the customer receiving the value that they expect and are willing to pay for?

Each part of the DMAIC process has its own set of unique tools and the *measure phase* is no different. Some of these such as the measurement system analysis can become quite technical; however, from an educational perspective there is one primary tool that will guide us on our journey to educational excellence. In the *define stage* we discussed the creation of a process map for your recruitment process. At this point we need to return to that discussion.

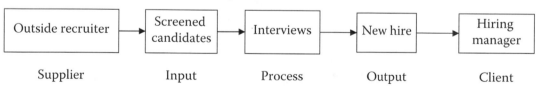

| Supplier | Input | Process | Output | Client |

The process map is a review of how you do things from an eagle's point of view. It is performed from a point above the organization to see how a process works its way through the organization. It applies to either a whole organization or a single department on an equal basis. The process map also does not allow for the introduction of the required data points.

In the *measure stage* we bring this eagle's view down to the ground level and expand the pictorial view presented by the process map. The tool that we use in this instance is a value stream map. Look at the process map shown previously. From this point we are going to take it to the next level. The value stream map looks at every part of the recruitment process from the perspective of the Ishikawa Fishbone Cause and Effect Diagram. When you convert your process map to a value stream map, we include every step and process included in the recruitment process. This includes people and materials such as documents, forms, online systems, and so on. It also includes the duration of lapsed time between each block or step. Following the completion of the value stream map, the organization creates a true picture of what it takes to hire an individual into your organization.

In one of the presentations of our seminar, driving the HR 500: Achieving HR excellence through Six Sigma, we had in the audience the HR manager, the recruiter and, the benefits coordinator. They completed the development of a value stream map of their recruitment process. When it was completed the HR director remarked: are we really pending that much time on this process. The time spent was there it just was hidden because they had never looked at it in detail.

An additional benefit of the *measure stage* is that it provides support for the establishment of KPIs. I had discussed that every process has its KPIs, which tell the organization what is essential for the process to operate effectively. The value stream map is one step in identifying those KPIs. They provide the expected signs of success and are the basis of this stage. These KPIs are based on the VOC as to what they expect from your organization.

With the KPIs in place and your data assimilated, the last step of the *measure stage* is to enter the data into a control chart of some sort. We would suggest that one of the easiest tools to use is a histogram. The histogram is a pictorial view of your data designed to show whether the process meets the view of the customer.

The visual shown in Figure 4.5 is a histogram developed to show the frequency of compensation across an organization. They are designed to provide a summary of the data you have collected from the organization. Each bar is representative of a data point that was collected during the *measure stage*. Most of the Six Sigma-related software programs such as QI Macros contain a user-friendly histogram in which you need to basically fill in the blanks and it will draw the chart for you.

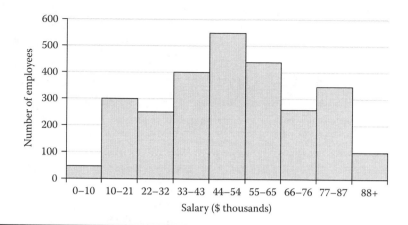

Figure 4.5 Compensation spread. (Image from http://haleysmaps.blogspot. com/2011/04/histogram.html.)

To this point we have defined our problem (i.e., defined our hypothesis) and we have undertaken efforts to collect data as to the performance of our processes. We have, in essence, tested whether our experiment proved or disproved what we thought the problem was. The next question becomes, what do we do with the data we have collected?

Analyze Stage

The scientific method tells us that we have to define our problem, arrive at a hypothesis or guesstimate of what the solution is, measure our data points, and then analyze the results. The DMAIC process is no different. At this point we have determined that we have a problem. We then take steps to collect the data points on the performance of the process in question and now we come to the next step. We now need to analyze the data to determine what the process is telling us.

The determination of what the data is telling your organization comes in the *analyze stage*. There is not a day that goes by that your organization does not collect an overload of data that is created by the very nature of the educational process. The downside to all this data is that, as we will see in Chapter 5, this overproduction of data is a type of non-value-added waste within your organization. In many cases, we collect data for some really good reason at the time, but where does that data end up residing:

It resides in that file drawer in your desk.
It sits on a shelf on the bookcase in your office.

*The reports are ordered by a member of management because they think
they need the data even if they have no use for the resulting reports.*

The DMAIC process sets five areas of concern when we are beginning
the *analyze stage*. Each of the areas of concern is asking us to challenge the
status quo and seeks to find the real outputs of the process in question.

Question 1: How Does the Process Perform?

As in the testing the hypothesis phase of the scientific method, one of the
outcomes of the methodology is to determine whether the results of our
experiments prove the hypothesis. In this case we are concerned with
whether or not the solution we suggested in the project charter actually
solves the elimination of the obstacle within our processes. One of the
benefits of the measurement stage, and thus the analysis stage, is that we
get to uncover hidden obstacles that are slowing down the process. The two
phases provide us with a visual picture of the process that is currently in
place. As stated earlier, using the tools of the analysis stage makes us view
the process in its entirety, to determine whether the mission of the process
is what we are delivering. For example, a hiring manager tells you that he
needs a suitable candidate in 2 days. Does the process allow the HR function to deliver on those terms?

Question 2: What Areas Are Causing the Problem?

My favorite statement to clients is if you have a process, then it will eventually
experience a hiccup. Guaranteed that it will happen. The critical question is,
can we identify those hiccups before they become a problem? Like the example we gave earlier of the organization that had a job requisition reviewed by
the same person three times, the *analysis phase* should seek out, locate, and
make the necessary adjustments allowing the process to run more effectively.
To achieve this goal we need to put the process under a microscope. We want
to view each and every step within the process to determine if what we are
doing is what the client needs and wants. If not, we have found the problem
area and in the next phase, we will correct the process going forward.

A real-time example can be found in the hiring process. The hiring manager calls your office with an urgent request. His lead IT person just walked
out the door and he desperately needs a replacement within 3 days. The HR
function does everything you are asked to do, but then the hiring manager

sits on the applications for 3 months. Has the process worked for your organization? Probably not, and more than likely, someone will scream that HR is not doing its job.

Question 3: What Does the Current State Show Us?

On the surface, when you look at the problem, is it indicating that the problem exists? Does the nature of the problem indicate what is responsible for the problem? Notice we did not ask who was responsible for the problem as the answer is never in the human capital assets but rather the way the process is constructed and unfolded. So our question becomes the client is telling us that there is a problem with some aspect of our way of delivering educational services to the client. We then are charged with finding out why the problem exists. The *analyze phase* concentrates our efforts in looking at what the process is delivering to the system and why it is causing the waste to occur.

Question 4: What Does the Data Indicate?

Part of the testing process is to confirm that the data collected is both creditable and verifiable. The data collected must be centered on the problem at hand. This is a good point to stress that we are not trying to solve every problem within the organization at one time. We are collecting data on the critical few problems that are affecting the organizational strategic initiatives. It is common for management to disavow that there are any problems. To them the organization is running smoothly. The problems arise when the client tells the organization that your service is not performing at the level they want and they may have to take their business elsewhere. Then we become forced into reviewing the process for where it is not meeting those needs.

Question 5: Does the Root Cause(s) Affect the VOC Issues?

In the *define stage* we discussed the Ishikawa Fishbone, in which we looked at the six elements of the corporate structure that are affected by the elements of the fishbone. Critically, we now need to review that diagram to ascertain what happens if we do this rather than do that. By gaining an understanding of the relationship between the diagram elements and the VOC we develop a better picture of how our strategic initiatives affect the process in the long run.

As you can observe from Figure 4.6, there are seven distinct tools that come into play within the *analyze stage*. Of these, three can have a

DMAIC step	Six Sigma tools	Lean tools
Define	Voice of customer Project charter Project critical to quality definition High-level process map	Value definition
Measure	Quality function deployment Measurement system analysis	Value stream mapping
Analyze	**Process capability analysis** **FMEA** **Benchmarking** **Hypothesis testing** **Graphical tools**	**Line balance** **Takt time calculation**
Improve	Regression analysis Design of experiments Risk assessment	5 S Establish flow/pull system SCORE events
Control	Determine new process capability Statistical process control Control plants	Poka Yoke Visual management

Figure 4.6   Six sigma methodology tool box: Analyze stage.

distinct role within educational processes. As educational professionals, you have been using the first of these for years. You just did not recognize it as part of the continuous process improvement effort. You are considering offering a new policy or curriculum. What is the first thing you do? Most of us would go to the groups we belong to and ask whether any of the members have implemented a similar program and how did you do it. This tool is called benchmarking. The purpose of the benchmarking process is to identify what went right and what went wrong when others tried to implement the same process. It also provides you with a roadmap to continuous process improvement steps necessary to successfully introduce the service through molding the process to represent what has worked in the past.

The second tool is the series of control charts, which can again be found in the QI Macros software. The data plots on the control chart indicate whether we are operating within the process limits that we have established. If the data analysis indicates we are operating within the process limits then we know that we are achieving the results we expected. If, however, the results are outside of the process limits, then we know we have a problem. The *analyze phase* then points out where we have to make changes to the process to bring it within the process limits.

The third and final tool is a concept called takt time. Takt time is a mathematical equation to determine the processing time to compete a process. It is calculated by completing the following formula:

$$\text{Takt time} = \text{Net available time available to work}$$
$$\text{divided by the customer demand}$$

In other words, the time it takes to complete the process is calculated by the amount of time available to work divided by the number of units per day requested by the customer. Wikipedia provides a good example[4] in which the example lays out the steps. See the following full example.

> If there is a total of 8 hours (or 480 minutes) in a shift (gross time) less 30 minutes lunch, 30 minutes for breaks (2×15 mins), 10 minutes for a team briefing and 10 minutes for basic maintenance checks, then the net Available Time to Work $= 480 - 30 - 30 - 10 - 10 = 400$ minutes. If customer demand was, say, 400 units a day and one shift was being run, then the line would be required to spend a maximum of one minute to make a part in order to be able to keep up with customer demand.

Takt time can be used in calculating how long it will take to recruit a person depending on the hiring manager's requirements and the available time the recruiter has to source new candidates.

Improve Stage

Along with the *define stage*, the *improve stage* may very well be the most critical parts of the continuous improvement process as they set the tone for where we are and where the journey is headed.

In Chapter 2, the section on the modern day evolution of Six Sigma, I made reference to the Ultimate Improvement Cycle which is designed to identify the roadblocks or obstacles that hinder us meeting the VOC, to identify the causes of those roadblocks and remove them from the process. It is during this stage that we undertake the changes to the process that we are reviewing in the DMAIC process. It is also in this phase that we begin to accomplish the efforts to change the corporate culture in addition to the process.

We need to step back for a moment and consider the impact of the previous statement. Many continuous process improvement efforts fail because the organization looks for fast returns on the efforts or "quick fixes." The real success of the efforts we are discussing come about due to the organization changing, changes in the way we think about the organization, changes in the way we do things. Any successful improvement process involves a change in the cultural view of the organization. Not just for the moment, but for the long term. It requires the organization to change from an "our perspective" to one of the client perspective. What we do and how we do it must be centered on the concept of VOC mentioned several times so far in the book. The *improve stage* is where the focus needs to be established that any changes to the processes within the organization are totally focused on delivering only value-added services to the clients.

In the *improve stage*, the cross-functional team comes together and looks at the data and questions that have been answered to this point and using that information decide where the organization goes next on this journey. They do this through a review of the organization, the findings, and the available solutions. There are four distinct views that the cross-functional team would take to determine the next step.

1. *What alternative solutions are available?*
   Via the benchmarking process the cross-functional team more than likely has come up with a wide range of potential solutions to the problem at hand. While they all are potential solutions, they need to be viewed from the perspective of which ones would not add non-value-added waste into the existing process. If a certain solution does contribute to the waste within the system, then it is a necessity that it be dropped from the potential changes to the process.
2. *Which alternative solution(s) will meet the VOC issues the best?*
   This is the point where the culture of the organization comes into play. The cross-functional team may have come up with some really unique and exciting solutions to remove the process obstacles. However, when we take the culture of the organization into consideration, there are some of them that obviously would not work in your cultural environment. You may ask how we know in advance that something would not work within our organization. The real response to the question is how the organization feels about change. If there is a natural resilience to change from the functional silos, a dramatic change effort, most likely, would not work. When we are in these environments it requires a slower pace to

make the changes than when both management and rank and file fully support the need for changes in the way the organization functions.

3   *What's the downside of implementing the alternative solution selected?*

Face it, any time we make changes in the way we perform things within the organization it entails a sense of risk. Six Sigma and continuous process improvement are a risk issue. We know we have a problem, so what is the impact if we decide that we will leave the status quo in place? What is the impact to the organization if we do this? What is the impact of the change for the rank-and-file employee? We know we have a problem but is it a life-and-death environment if we choose to ignore the VOC? I would suggest that if we recognize that there is a problem the risk factor is greater on the organization if we do nothing. The current process is definitely demonstrating that the customer is not happy with the service they are receiving and they are left with two alternatives. One is to push to get us to change how we perform or the other is to move their business elsewhere. Both of these alternatives also carry risk. If the customer moves to another source there is no guarantee that things will be any better with the new vendor. If they stay put they are still not guaranteed that things will improve.

4.   *What is the process for implementing the selected solution(s)?*

Implementation of the chosen solution can have various outcomes. The outcomes are based on how and when we implement the solutions. You have a decision to make. On the one hand, you can implement it across the entire organization. This can be a major undertaking depending on the reaction from the employee base. This method has some really good evidence-based knowledge that it can work. This was the way Toyota implemented their process improvement efforts. The other option is to introduce into a single function or department. Let the function become the model for how to do it right and then using this model, roll it out to the rest of the organization.

As we enter the *improvement stage* (Figure 4.7), we should have at this point identified the problem, measured the data, and analyzed what it all means to the organization. There are several tools out of the toolbox that can help guide the process change. One of these is to change how we initiate both processes and the steps to completion. In many organizations the natural tendency is to operate from the belief that the best way for any function to make a contribution is to keep the pipeline fully loaded with talent or materials. The reason is the belief that if say the IT department needs a particular skill on an ongoing

DMAIC step	Six Sigma tools	Lean tools
Define	Voice of customer Project charter Project critical to quality definition High-level process map	Value definition
Measure	Quality function deployment Measurement system analysis	Value stream mapping
Analyze	Process capability analysis FMEA Benchmarking Hypothesis testing Graphical tools	Line balance Takt time calculation
Improve	**Regression analysis** **Design of experiments** **Risk assessment**	**5 S** **Establish flow/pull** **system** **SCORE events**
Control	Determine new process capability Statistical process control Control plants	Poka Yoke Visual management

Figure 4.7   Six sigma methodology tool box: Improve stage.

basis, then if HR continually pushes candidates to the IT department, when the time comes the staffing effort is already taken care of. The drawback is that some of the candidates may not be currently available. The alternative is to set up the process so that the hiring manager only receives information on potential candidates when the IT department requests it. We refer to this as a push vs. a pull environment. In the push environment the system is consistently filled with potential candidates while in the pull environment the only candidates in the pipeline are those requested for an actual opening.

There is one other scenario we need to consider at this point in our review. We have followed all the steps of the DMAIC process to this point. At the conclusion of the *analysis stage,* we discover that because of the way the process behaves none of the possible solutions will achieve the results we are seeking. The question then becomes, what do we do next? Six Sigma methodologies contain a different process for resolving this issue. It is called Design for Six Sigma (DSS). Similar to when we are looking at an existing process, DSS has its own process steps. While we will not do a deep dive into the DSS process, as it is outside of the approach this book is taking, we do want you to be knowledgeable of the steps in the process. It is much like designing an experiment in science.

From the book *Design for Six Sigma for Service*[5] we can see that there are some strikingly similarities in the DSS process. DSS is divided into five phases resulting in the introduction of the new process within the organization.

In Phase 1, we define the existing problem. It begins with defining the problem through a project charter to lay out the problem as we did in the DMAIC process. Since we are creating a new process, we next need to identify the customers that will receive the most benefit from this new process. With the customer in mind we create a process map of the future state of the new process, laying out the development states. It works exactly the way we did earlier in this chapter.

Based on the charter and the process map we then decide what metrics we need to confirm that the process will achieve our expected outcome.

Phase 2 measures the determined metric and how they perform in the new process. This is very much like testing our hypothesis in both the scientific method and the DMAIC process. We are going to handle the metric performance identically to the DMAIC and can use the same tools as we did previously. The results lead us to identifying the performance metrics that meet the voice of the customer.

Phase 3 analyzes the current process by running a process diagnosis on the current process with the assistance of tools such as a value stream map. It is from the first two phases and the resulting analysis that we are able to begin the design of creditable alternative solutions to the existing process.

Phase 4 the cross-functional team designs the brand-new solution. It takes into consideration all of the data that has been gathered and lays out the steps to reach the ultimate outcome. One useful tool is run simulations of the process alternatives to determine the best solution to the organizational problem.

In the final phase we are confronted with a lack of information to complete the last step of the DMAIC process. We have nothing to improve, nor do we have something to necessarily control. To finalize the process, we need to verify that the new solution to the problem is in fact working and resolving the customer problem with the current process.

Control Stage

The final goal of the DMAIC process is to create a standard of work that governs the way the process is delivered going forward. The standard of work is not a guide on how to do something necessarily. It is, however, a roadmap for the organization as to how a process should be delivered. It is an organization process map to respond to the VOC. Take, for example, the recruitment process, as we have done throughout this book, and look at not how we recruit new talent but what steps we take to do so. This is the standard of work.

In order to create the standard of work, it is critical that the cross-functional team and the organization have a session devoted to critiquing the DMAIC process. We would suggest that this can be accomplished by responding to four questions.

First, just because we have completed the five stages of the continuous process improvement stage does not mean that our review is over. Notice that when we talk about the DMAIC we make reference to *continuous* process improvement. This is not a one-time event so how is the process going to be measured after the project is completed? Understand that the chances that you are going to need to revisit the process in the near future are fairly strong, so what are you going to look for and how are you going to determine if it meets the ongoing needs of all stakeholders.

Second, we discussed previously that continuous process improvement and Six Sigma are a change agents. You will not successfully implement the process improvements without a change in the organizational culture. We can provide an example of this by turning to the training and development space within most organizations. We spend large amounts of monies to send employees to a wide variety of training programs. When they return to the office, the manager typically tells the employee the training probably was helpful but returns you to the way you have always done it to get through the work that has amassed while you were gone. This is not a change in corporate culture. It is absolutely essential that the improvements to our organizational processes must become the new business as usual, not just within the functional area where the process resides but throughout the entire organization. The process changes must be understood and implemented from the superintendent to the classroom.

Third, in the project charter one of the last sections asks us to describe what we believe the project impact would be on the total organization. In the *control phase* we take some time out to compare that impact statement to the reality of the process results. If we stated that we would reduce costs by $100,000 did we actually save the organization that much. The impact statement also should have described other changes within the post-organizational space and now we have to determine whether we, in fact, met those goals also.

Fourth, in the project charter we established milestones for this project. These milestones were deliverables that arose out of our efforts. The last of these milestones should have established a date in the future when the final reports were to be delivered to management. At this point we need to look at the project charter and the Gantt charter and determine whether we will meet that milestone target. Part of the *control stage* is for the team to review the process and see if you were able to complete the steps you set out to cover in the time frame you predicted (Figure 4.8). Process improvement projects are never open ended; they always have a set beginning date and ending date.

As we stated at the beginning of this chapter, we are trying to establish a standard of work for our educational processes. The *control stage* gives us several tools to assist in the development of that standard.

First, we can create control plans. A control plan is a document that describes for the organization the information about the process in play. It informs the user the name of the process, what machines are used, the allowable tolerance from the standard, and how you are going to measure the process going forward. It further discusses what control method is in place to ensure that the standard of work is followed.

The second tool is called visual management. Using a large whiteboard you can create a visual process map that hangs on the wall. In an article that appeared in the *Human Resource Executive* entitled "Lean and Mean,"[6] GE Healthcare described how they created a giant whiteboard which was divided into sections which corresponded to the steps in their standard of

DMAIC step	Six Sigma tools	Lean tools
Define	Voice of customer Project charter Project critical to quality definition High-level process map	Value definition
Measure	Quality function deployment Measurement system analysis	Value stream mapping
Analyze	Process capability analysis FMEA Benchmarking Hypothesis testing Graphical tools	Line balance Takt time calculation
Improve	Regression analysis Design of experiments Risk assessment	5 S Establish flow/pull system SCORE events
Control	**Determine new process capability** **Statistical process control** **Control plants**	**Poka Yoke** **Visual management**

Figure 4.8 Six sigma methodology tool box: Control stage.

work called recruitment. On the chart they posted Post-it notes for each candidate involved in the process. As the candidate progressed through the process, his or her Post-it was moved to the next stage. Any member of the HR staff or management could look at the board and immediately tell whether there was some bottleneck which was holding up the hiring of the required new talent.

The third tool for the *control stage* is a Japanese term called Poka Yoke. Remember the goal of this phase is the creation of a standard of work, and the ultimate goal is to have that standard be what comes to play every time that you initiate the process. Poka Yoke is intended to make the standard of work mistake proof. It means setting up your work stations so that everything has its place, and it is clearly marked where that location is. For example if you needed a I-9 form to be completed by a new hire, the form could be found in a specific labeled location within the HR workspace.

Summary

This chapter carefully created a picture of how the Six Sigma methodology works in your organization. Comparing the methodology to the scientific method learned in high school science classes, we have shown that there is a discipline that is followed to explore how our delivery to the end user is either flawed or is not meeting the needs of the customer. A point visited again in further chapters is that this entire effort is not people oriented, meaning that the reason why we have a problem is never because the human capital messed up. If there is a hiccup in any process, it is the process that is the cause of the error. The purpose of the methodology is to identify the obstacle, remove it, and ensure that we follow the standard of work going forward. Anytime we deviate from the standard of work we are creating waste.

In the next chapter, I will explore the types of waste that can appear within your organization.

Notes

1. Wikipedia. Scientific Method. http://en.wikipedia.org/wiki/Scientific_method.
2. Mikel, H. and Schroeder, R. *Six Sigma: The Breakthrough Management Strategy Revolutionizing the World's Top Corporations.* New York: Crown Publishing, 2005.

3. Gantt charts can be found within MS Project or use another software platform such as Fast Track Scheduler from AEC Software.
4. http://en.wikipedia.org/wiki/Takt_time.
5. Yang, Kai. *Design for Six Sigma for Service.* New York: McGraw-Hill, 2005. Pp. 42–46.
6. *Human Resource Executive Magazine.* Lean and Mean, LRP Publications, March 16, 2009. http://www.hreonline.com/HRE/story.jsp?storyid=18721619&query=GE Healthcare.

Chapter 5

In Plain Sight: Sources of Wastes

Visit any business enterprise or residential home in the global space and you will find in each case that there is a process in place to remove waste from the location. We are talking about those items that most municipalities call solid waste. However, this chapter is not concerned with those items that are headed for the landfill. That is not our working definition of waste[1] in the pursuit of excellence within the schools.

In the previous chapter I discussed in detail the DMAIC method of searching out problems that affect our organizations. Further explored were the ways our organizations can strive to remove the roadblocks or obstacles from these processes. At the same time, we are trying to create a standard of work by removing the inherent variations which might be present in the process. In this chapter we are going to look at wastes that are found within the educational processes. This does not mean solid waste but rather those steps that have been added to any of your processes that are not of direct value to the internal or external customer.

Consider your instructional process to bring innovation into your organization as an example. Our organizations have been very good at adding steps to the process, whether it is from the suggestion of upper management or someone in the stakeholder space who felt that the new step would assist the process. Many of the steps have been added without consultation with their customers, internal or external. I would assert that if we were able to look at any organization in existence throughout the global workplace, there would not be a single organization that did not contain waste of some sort. In fact, Jay Arthur of KnowledgeWare suggests that for every $100 of corporate spend in a 3-Sigma corporation, $25–$40 of it is wasteful spending.[2]

Shigeo Shingo and Taiichi Ohno, looking at the production of an automobile on the Toyota Production System, indicated that until the final bolt was subjected to the wrench everything else was movement. Whenever you have any form of movement within your process, you are subjected to the potential for the inclusion of non-value-added steps to be introduced. Toyota and the Toyota Production System suggested that every organization actually has present three types of waste. The first is *MUDA*,[3] which refers to those wastes that utilize human activity but do not add value to the customer requirements. The second is *MURI*, which refers to actions by the organization that add unreasonable expectations on the organization, and the final type is *MURA*, which refers to variation and inconsistency within the organization. While it may not meet all our needs it is simpler to lump all the wastes together under the MUDA umbrella, but we need to clarify a concept before continuing. By the term waste, we are not referring to something that when it is found within the organization is taken out to the back of the facility and placed in a container for the waste management company to retrieve. We are not talking about wrapping from food or products purchased for the organization.

The original set of waste categories contained seven areas found in almost every organization. In the course of the ensuing pages we will look at the original seven plus two additional ones that many professionals now include—nine[4] in detail (Figure 5.1).

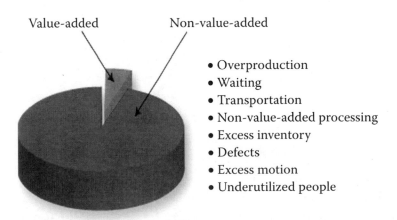

Figure 5.1   Nine areas of waste within the marketplace.

Waste Type 1: Overproduction

As human beings, we have a tendency to believe more is better in the long run. The result is that we get a request for data and we tend to produce way more than the customer asked for or needs. Ohno suggested that this was the worst kind of waste as its implementation tends to hide the other eight types of waste.[5]

Consider these examples from a real-time school environment. Each of these can be found in every school in the country and even potentially in every school globally.

Excess requisitions: Consider this scenario. You are an instructional professional, and to meet the state requirements you need to secure a textbook or a resource to complete that requirement. Along come the school policies, which require the instructional personnel to complete multiple copies of the material requisition with one going to the department chairman, one to the administration, one to the finance people and, one to go to the procurement people. A requisition that is required by the school procurement process creates waste based on the number of copies required.

Creation of too much information: As an educational institution we are directly responsible to our stakeholders whether it is the public or the parents, in the case of a private school. The tendency when we get pushed by these outside parties to justify what we do is to overproduce the evidence-based data to support the request. When we create data in excess of what is required to support the request, we have created waste.

Creation of excess reports: In the same vein as too much information, the tendency is to go beyond what is required by the stakeholder requirements to present information in response to requests. For example, you might be requested to provide reports about the performance of a section of your student body, but you provide a report of all segments of the student body. Excess reports are waste.

Excess data retrieval: Whether you are talking about a business organization or a school, we find overzealous human capital assets who tend to go overboard. A request is made for data pertaining to, say, the last report card period, and the final report delivers information for last year and the current report card. The creation of excess data that is not needed by the customer is waste.

Waste Type 2: Waiting

The second form of non-value-added activities or waste is that of waiting. It refers to the tendency of organizations to put off what they need to do even when there is a deadline in place. Many reasons are given for the delay; however, any time we delay the delivery of a product or service beyond when the customer requests it is waste. As previously, consider these examples:

Undefined decision-making: Ask almost any professional involved in our educational systems and you are likely to hear about situations that demand an answer to a problem, and no one seems to be able to come up with a decision. The school principal can't give you an answer. The district or school trustees can't give you an answer. Everyone responds "it is not my job."

Fill times: It is the beginning of the school year, and requests have been made for textbooks or other resources for the start of the year. The final hour is at hand, and either the textbooks have not arrived or the resources are missing. When the required resources are not present when they are needed, we have produced waste.

Customer unmet needs: There is a constant demand from our stakeholders for better-prepared human capital assets for the future. We hear of employers complaining that the talent market is lacking the skills to meet the needs of the future jobs. The expectation is that the schools will bring those skills to the market. When we don't, we have created waste.

Waste Type 3: Unnecessary Transport

Ever worked in an organization where it seems they re-arrange the office every time the wind changes? Many times there is a valid reason for the changes. Other times it is supposed to be to meet some reported need. The problem is that sometimes the movement creates more problems than believed because the total organization was not reviewed.

Unnecessary movement: Many educational systems have taken great strides in making the efficiencies of the school operations designed to enhance the operations of both the classroom and the administration.

School flow: You are in your classroom and need to get to the front office. Can you get there in an easy trip? If you are like most people you develop a standard path to get somewhere. Do you still follow that path if it means that you expend extra time to get there based on your path?

Waste Type 4: Overprocessing

A member of the administration attends a conference and hears of a new strategy within the educational arena and comes back to the school and implements it without seeing how it will fit into the total educational system. Somewhere back in time a minor crisis occurred, and the administration decides that to avoid it happening again they will implement oversight controls on the educational system (the classroom as well as the administrative function). All of these could be great ideas, but if they are not taken in the context of your corporate culture you are asking for added problems. These added steps were implemented to isolate the organization but not to meet the needs of the customer. Consider these examples where good ideas went bad:

Excess steps in the hiring process: Schools are no different from many corporations in the marketplace. You have an automated, online applicant tracking system, and yet when you schedule an interview you ask the candidate to fill out a paper application. Waste occurs whenever we add steps to a process that are not critical to the success of the process.

Redundancy: In every organization, and schools are not an exception to the rule, redundancy is a fact of life. We place orders for new equipment when the same equipment is sitting unused in our supply closets. We have resources around the schools that are never catalogued, but when we need them we forget they are in the school already.

Island mentality: Constantly we find in organizations people who respond to issues by saying "it is not my job." Let me share a personal episode. When I graduated out of college I went to work for two Catholic schools in a midwestern city. One of the policies was that students were not to skip the stairs from the cafeteria to the playground. One day I was walking down from the cafeteria and a student decided to skip the stairs. The process said when caught the student was supposed to be sent back to the top of the stairs and made to walk down the way that was expected. As a result I told the student to go back upstairs, and when he did he met up with the principal/nun. She immediately came down and told me I did not have the right to tell the student to rewalk the stairs. We have a tendency to feel that we are in a bubble, and the world around that bubble does not exist.

Waste Type 5: Excess Inventory

Wikipedia defines excess inventory as a capital outlay in which there is no return from the customer. We usually consider this from the point of view of a physical item. However, you can also have excess inventory from a service prospective. From the educational perspective we are talking about the accumulation of too much stuff.

Too much work in progress: In the education world, this comes to life in a huge assortment of demands on the instructional professional's day. Requests from the parents. Requests from the administrators. Requests from the state legislators. The compilation of all the requests can lead to an increased level of work expectations. When, as we will see later in this book, we are confronted with too many requests, we create waste.

Physical pile of forms: Just like businesses, the tendency is that many schools estimate the supply of forms they need even though the estimate is unrealistic. The waste is created when you revise the form and you are stuck with an excess in the number of forms left when you revise them. What do you do with them?

Waste Type 6: Unnecessary Movement

In virtually every corporate facility in the world, if we utilize the spaghetti diagram tool or the Stand in a Circle tool created from Ohno,[6] we can see that we have designed the work floor not entirely in the most efficient way to move human capital within the system. The added steps required to complete the process based on the workflow create waste as we create less productivity. The same can be applied to the educational organizations. Some real-life examples of this can be found in the following:

Needless switching of programs: You are working on a lesson plan or analyzing a bunch of figures in an Excel spreadsheet, and suddenly an administrator calls and wants information out of either a report or another spreadsheet. How many steps to you have to take to switch programs on your screen in front of you? Can you view the other program without closing down the first program?

Needless movement of people: As organizations, we tend to make a lot of our decisions on impulse. We set up office space in ways that may not make sense in real time. Part of this trend is the way we construct our schools. We talked earlier about the use of spaghetti diagrams, which map the traffic flow through a plant floor or an office area. Many times the diagram shows us that part of the traffic patterns fails at the logic of the flow. The waste comes from the waste of time in moving illogically through the school when you could be teaching or ordering supplies that administration or instructors have requested.

Needless movement of information: Your customer asks for a certain report, and you generate the report only to find out that the manager did not need the report after all. I recently talked with a CPA who stated that one of his staff had generated a financial report for a client only to have the report end up sitting on a bookshelf within the CPA's office. The movement of information that has no importance to the customer is waste.

Waste Type 7: Defects

This could easily be the largest segment of the waste types and includes many easily overlooked examples of non-value-added steps in the educational arena. Many of these defects may be simple slips as part of being human, but they do represent waste in the system. It refers to construction projects that do not meet the milestones for completion. It refers to those opportunities where the wrong information is provided and the result is a disruption to the student or stakeholders. Consider these further examples:

1. Student report card is due for release, but the grade is computed inaccurately.
2. The School Board of Trustees issues a new policy, and the implementation does not go as planned due to faulty communication pieces.
3. The school procurement office places order with a publisher for some textbooks, and the publisher sends less than the order.
4. In 2014, John Hopkins University issued 300 letters of acceptance to students applying for admission that did not meet the cut off criteria for admission.

Waste Type 8: Unused Employee Potential

Can any of you remember the Negro College Fund's slogan that "a mind is a terrible thing to waste"? While this was referring to the opportunities for a young African American trying to get through higher education, the same question can be posed to the internal organization and how you treat your human capital. We can waste the contributions of our human capital assets when we place them in less than optimal work environments. For example,

> *Understaffing:* The school enrollment dramatically increases but the number of instructors does not likewise increase.
>
> *Overstaffing:* A local school district found that they were short on funds and brought in a consultant who concluded that in the end that they had hired 1700 more teachers than was needed based on the current population.
>
> *No time for continuing education:* The expectation is that all instructional staff will work toward additional education to further their educational career, but then we add on additional demands from the other side of the coin to the point where teachers only have time to teach, complete testing, and file the necessary statistical data for reports on school progress.

Waste Type 9: Material Underutilization

The last of the nine types of wastes is that of material underutilization, and it refers to how we use materials within the organization. Every day we do things within the organizational structure that create waste in the processes and organization such as

Emails: Are you one who believes they have to keep every email? Do you get in to school in the morning and proceed to make copies of every email in the inbox?

Late arrivals: Do you have a meeting scheduled and you find some reason for being late to the start? This is waste. This is lost productivity time, costing the school time and money.

Design errors: How many times have you made up communication or instructional materials and placed only two copies of the item when the sheet being used would make four? The scrap when you cut out the white space around each item is waste.

Notes

1. http://en.wikipedia.org/wiki/Muda_%28Japanese_term%29.
2. Arthur, Jay. *Free, Perfect and Now.* Denver, CO: KnowledgeWare, 2012. P. 18.
3. www.1000ventures.com/business_guide/lean_waste_3typcs.html.
4. http://asq.org/quality-progress/2010/08/one-good-idea/number-nine.html.
5. http://en.wikipedia.org/wiki/Muda_%28Japanese_term%29.
6. The Stand in a Circle tool requires managers to stand in a circle and view the reality of the business environment for a period of at least 25 minutes. The question is, what do you see wrong?

Chapter 6

Transforming the Educational System

If you are still reading this book at this point, I am glad you are beginning to get the message. Some of you may have asked "why we have not talked about real-time applications until this point?" I understand that inclination. The title of the book is transforming the schools. I promise that in the next four chapters I will provide the information that you are seeking.

Before we get there it would be appropriate to review how we got to this point and cover one final concept, which will play out in our discussions of the instructional and operational sides of the educational system.

In Chapter 1, the discussion was centered on how we defined the term educational excellence. Typically, our definition of excellence in education seems to be centered on the anticipated student outcome. However, I expressed the view that any accepted definition needed to go beyond just how we prepared the student to look at the totality of the quality efforts. In the next chapters we will discuss examples of schools that have adopted this extended definition.

In Chapter 2, our direction turned to developing an evolutionary journey map of the quality movement that was intended to expose you to the thinking of the quality thought leaders on how to develop the quality measurements within your organization.

In Chapter 3, I discussed the TLS Continuum toolbox and how we apply the tools to the problem-solving efforts to resolve your organizational problems. The methodology clearly lays out the step-by-step system to understand what is involved with the issues that are confronting the system.

As I stated already, we have one more concept before we begin to look at how to transform the schools. A college classmate of mine, Dr. Lawrence Miller, developed the concept of the whole system architecture.[1] It begins with the question, what is a system?

The *Theory of Constraints Handbook*[2] defines a system as being made up of inputs, a process of some kind, outputs, and the environment in which these components exist. So let's dissect the key components of the definition. The first component is that it requires inputs of some sort. Your stakeholders are the ones that bring the inputs to the table. The inputs are designed to furnish or provide (a person, establishment, place, etc.) with what is lacking or requisite in the completion of a process. The second component is that there must be a process in place. I reviewed this in our discussions in Chapter 4 in looking at the methodology when you were asked to review the process maps and the value stream maps. Each process has a beginning and an end result. The fourth component is the presence of outputs. As I explained in the discussion of the SIPOC at the beginning of Chapter 4, if we have something flow into the organization, which serves as the fuel for a process, we must as a matter of recourse have something flow out of the process. We do not enter into any process without expecting something to result from the completion of that process. It is the intention that the output is the deliverable to your customer.

The final element of the system definition is that it must exist within an environment of some sort. In particular, the environment in our discussion is the educational institution that we all live and work in every day. You work in a tough environment, but it is still embedded in processes from both the instructional and the operational sides of the coin.

I need to digress a bit and consider your outlook on process improvement within your organization. There is an ongoing debate in the quality efforts as to where our energies should be directed. Do we only look at making the educational organization more Lean or efficient? Do we only look at making the educational organization more effective via the Six Sigma methodology? I would propose to you, why would you look at only a third of the pie? Many of you will follow recipes that have been handed down over generations in your families. But what if someone came to you and said "This year why don't you only make a third of a pie?" Sound ridiculous? How would you respond to the request? I expect that most of you would say you can't comply with the request. We in essence ask the same question when we make the statement we only do Lean or we only do Six Sigma. This is like cooking a third of a pie. Let me explain the argument.

In my September (2013) article in *QHSE Magazine*, I introduced the concept of the TLS Continuum. It is a continuum that comprises the three parts of the pie.

The first third of the pie is the identification of the process obstacle. What is the process component that is holding up the complete delivery of the ultimate goal? The Theory of Constraints (TOC) tells us what needs to change, what to change it to, and how to make the change happen. Basically, the TOC slice of the pie enables us to identify through strategic thinking tools what the problem is that we are experiencing. From there, the critical thinking tools identify what the critical success factors are to reach the goal of removing the obstacle. We cannot just go out into the community and say we have this goal to remove obstacle X without identifying what will tell us that we have reached the goal. These two steps are necessary but not sufficient, however, without a detailed look at the conditions that must be present to create the critical success factors. The first part of the pie therefore lays the ground work for the remainder of the system of continuous improvement. We have, essentially, met the first part of the TLS goal of delivery of the product or service faster, better, and cheaper. We have identified how to make the end result *better* with a higher level of quality.

The second slice of the pie is Lean. Productivity Press's *Lean Speak*[3] defines Lean as a system "that has relatively little non-value adding waste and maximum flow." It is the second part of the pie that delivers the end product or service *faster*. The primary function of Lean is to remove the obstacle and the accompanying waste. The obstacle that we identified in the TOC stage is slowing down the system due to the inability of the system to deliver the voice of the customer when they need the service delivered. This can occur because the process has added steps which made sense to someone but do not to the customer. This can occur because we have introduced to the system demands that overtax the system causing longer delivery times.

The final third of the pie is that of Six Sigma. The intent of Six Sigma is to ensure that our processes meet three criteria. First, the problem-solving method creates a standard of work. We do not remove the ability of an organization to innovate, as this is critical for organizational competiveness in today's marketplace. It does, however, put in place a system that is the same every time we begin to complete the process. If we are going to hire a new human capital asset for the organization, the hiring process components are the same each and every time. One of the characteristics of a Six Sigma process is that it is repeatable. The second part of the process is that it is creditable. This means that the data we use to implement the change is based on verifiable data from the operation. One of the ways we achieve this is through removing the variations from the process. By following the steps outlined here, we ensure that waste does not creep back into the process. This would meet the final part of the pie, that we reduce costs, not to produce the product or service but by delivering it sooner to the end user.

The TLS Continuum focuses on continuously improving the transactional process quality, getting the product or service to market faster, and reducing cost while improving the price to the customer. It is the total pie that delivers the promise of the continuum to produce measurable continuous process improvement.

There is an axiom in the scientific community stating that the sum of the parts is greater than each contribution of the parts. Thus, when we make the observation that we only use TOC, or Lean or Six Sigma, at the expense of the rest of the pie, we are not delivering the ultimate capability of the process. We are approaching the continuous process improvement arena as if we are baking only a third of a pie. Stop and think for a moment, and consider whether you are serving your customer by meeting his or her demands with only a third of the box of tools. You owe it to your customers and to your educational organization to deliver the total package.

My process obstacle in writing this book was, what was the single clear playing field that I could utilize that answered two questions?

The first question is, what are the key performance indicators (KPIs), which regardless of the level of experience, would be understood by most professionals in the educational field? While the KPIs will be different in the classroom compared to the operational side, they are just as critical for us to identify before we can bring about the change we are trying to accomplish. The process begins with the establishment of the suggested solution to the process improvement. As Dettmer suggested in his goal tree,[5] once we have set the goal it is then necessary that we determine what the critical factors necessary to achieve those solutions (goals) are. The critical success factors become the KPIs.

In today's volatile environment regarding the success of our education programs for the student population, which is centered on the results of standard testing, we need analytics to support our responses. We responded to the second question when we were able to identify evidence-based, creditable, and verifiable data. Evidence-based data that is verifiable and based on real data numbers.

In Chapters 7 and 8, I have given you some insight into the analytics that the methodology creates as we progress through the continuous improvement process. In Chapter 7, the focus is on examples of where the TLS Continuum has been used in the instructional environment. These examples are based on the belief that the use of instructional tools is, in itself, a process. In Chapter 8, I turn the focus to the operational side of the organization. I have found overwhelming examples of a dozen school districts, primarily from the Midwest section of this country, who utilize the TLS Continuum in an ongoing effort every day of the year. These examples will be presented via case studies of those that have found results that elevate their schools to new levels of performance and productivity.

Notes

1. Miller, Lawrence. http://www.lmmiller.com/wp-content/uploads/2011/06/Whole-System-Architecture-Article1.pdf.
2. Cox, James, and John Schleier, Jr. *Theory of Constraints Handbook*. New York: McGraw-Hill. P. 552.
3. Productivity Press. *Lean Speak*. New York: Productivity Press, 2002.
4. Dettmer, H. William. *The Logical Thinking Process*. Milwaukee, WI: ASQ Quality Press, 2007.

Chapter 7

TLS Continuum and the Classroom

In Chapter 1, I asked you for your thoughts on how we define educational excellence. In this chapter and the following chapter, we take a careful review of the definition in real time. Dr. Eliyahu Goldratt wrote a book titled *Necessary But Not Sufficient*.[1] And while the school needs the administration to make the system run smoothly, it is not sufficient to ensure the success of the system without the dedicated assistance of the trained educational professionals in the classroom. With that in mind, it is paramount that along with the definition of educational excellence we also need to understand what the purpose of the classroom effort is.

There have been many views as to the purpose of the classroom. The renowned philosopher Noam Chomsky, in *Parenting Magazine's* "What is the Purpose of Education,"[2] suggests that "education is aimed at helping students get to the point where they can learn on their own." In that same article, John Dewey is paraphrased as stating that "the general purpose of school is to transfer knowledge and prepare young people to participate in America's democratic society." More precisely, Dewey[3] stated "the primary purpose of education and schooling is not so much to *prepare* students to live a useful life, but to teach them how to live pragmatically and *immediately* in their current environment."

These definitions of educational purpose provide the foundation for a discussion of the legacy school versus the transformed school. Each can be found in our nation's schools, with the legacy school making up the vast majority of schools.

Legacy Classroom

What do we mean by the term legacy schools? Legacy schools comprise about 90% of the schools in the United States. They are schools that are based on the original concept of education developed by the first school in the United States, the Boston Latin School,[4] founded in 1635 by a group of business owners in the colonies. The legacy schools have been created on the premise that there is a standard body of knowledge that needs to be delivered to each student. This body of knowledge is divided into a standard of work, based on age and grade level, which prescribes what and how the body of knowledge is to be presented.

As the role of the administration is necessary but not sufficient to the transformed schools, the old standard is not sufficient to transform the schools. The idea of this standard of educational work dates back to the early 2000s with the introduction of a report that led to the creation of the common core.[5]

This standard, this way of working, was very much present when I entered college in the late 1960s to train to be a teacher. We were instructed that we had to master this body of knowledge which in turn had to be mastered by the individual student in order for them to progress on the educational journey to the next grade level. It was further instilled in us that there was only one true way to deliver material. This standard delivery was demonstrated in our daily and weekly lesson plans, which were reviewed by our department heads and/or principals. We have taken the legacy school to the next level, if you will, in that that standard of work means that we expect teachers to teach to the test. This new standard leaves us with students who don't remember what it was like to be a child. We are left with a segment of the population that does not know how to critically think. It is not enough to know that it is not working; we also need to know why it is not working.

Does this scenario sound even remotely familiar? We see it every day in our schools and in our corporations. The message to our students and to our human capital assets is that there is only one way to complete a task, and any deviation is prohibited. I can provide two examples of this in play. The first is back to the late 1970s, when I got into a rather heated discussion with a school principal who objected to my teaching methods in science for 8th graders. She claimed that she knew better than me how to teach science because she had taught science 25 years earlier. She believed that the required lesson plans and curriculum was the authority vehicle, and everything had to be done exactly that way.

The second example comes from my discussions with over 50 education professionals for this book. In one case the professional in question stated that when he was submitting his thesis for his doctorate, he described the ideas we will be discussing in the next several pages, and while the ideas sounded great, the school board determined they would continue the way they have always done it.

The downfall of these two examples is that the legacy standard of work did not work. This method of instilling the body of knowledge results in students who lack the ability to experiment as they did as young children. We are presented with students who either do not understand or are not motivated to perform experiments. In fact, they are left with a preparation effort that removes the ability to critically think. Not only do they not understand why something is not working, they may have a hard time understanding that it is not working. Instead, they are taught by rote and expected to master the skills that Dewey talked about.

Transformed Classroom

What is it that this new classroom environment brings to the equation? How does it differ from the legacy classroom? In case there is some misunderstanding, I am in no way advocating that the educational institutions eliminate the core body of knowledge or the curriculum. It is absolutely necessary that we have a clear picture of the direction that is needed. The community demands it. The business leaders demand it when they can't find human capital with the prerequisite skills. What has changed is the focus of the transformed classroom. What has changed is the method in which we present that curriculum. I need to have you, as the reader, open your eyes and ears and understand the potential for what I am about to present to you in the pages that follow.

Our business leaders tell us that they have a talent shortage. The shortage is not in the number of available bodies to fill positions. The shortage is in the skills that our human capital conveys to the organizations. Part of the responsibility for this condition resides in the legacy classroom.

Our legacy classroom is losing its way. The result is that the global business world is losing its way. Instead of contributing members of the business team we are creating a global workforce of robots. Instead of contributing members of the business team we are creating a global workforce that can state what they have learned by rote but not express the understanding behind the thought. The standard curriculum is taught in the same way and fashion no matter where you reside. The result is that our organizations lack the ability to innovate and deliver less than maximum performance.

So what is the missing element in the transformed classroom? What is missing in the transformed classroom is first, the ability to use critical thinking skills and then effective communication skills.

The Critical Thinking Community[6] defines it as that "mode of thinking—about any subject, content, or problem—in which the thinker improves the quality of his or her thinking by skillfully analyzing, assessing, and reconstructing it." When the student finishes the analysis of the problem, he or she can assess the impact on the organization and then reconstruct the process with inclusion of his or her solutions. This does not mean that management says "do this" and, like the aforementioned robots, we blindly follow along. It means we need to take the time and effort to accept the problems as a starting point and then, through the use of cross-functional teams, develop a solution to the problem based on careful consideration of all of the factors. Part of that cross-functional team environment is that the team needs to be able to communicate the problem, the solutions, and the logic behind the chosen direction.

To better understand the direction in which the transformed classroom needs to change and the strategies behind them, it is necessary to review the characteristics of the transformed classroom.

Creating Constancy of Purpose

The first step is that transformed classrooms must create a constant purpose of doing what is necessary to improve the classroom environment. Taking into consideration the history of the educational institution dating back to the Boston Latin School, we need to also look at what the future holds and what we need to do to get there. As teachers in a transformed classroom, we must be open to innovation both in the way we teach and the way we operate in the global workplace.

The second step is to adopt a new philosophy toward education. The new curriculum needs to be centered on the trio of concepts for problem solutions. The transformed classroom teacher must guide the students to understand that the process begins with the students being able to see the problem. Once the problem is recognized, the students through the acquisition of critical thinking skills must be able to recognize how the problem is affecting the organization. With these factors in place, they then need to be able to recommend responsible solutions to the problem. Their goal is to learn how to make the organization strive toward doing things faster, better, and cheaper.

There is a critical key to obtaining this new philosophy. Peter Senge in his book *Schools that Learn*[7] talks about having a shared vision for the transformed classroom and the use of system thinking in the way we present the subject matter. Both are critical to the adoption of the new philosophy. In the case studies at the end of the chapter you will see how these two factors work together. The use of the TLS Continuum within the transformed classroom must encompass everyone who has a stake in the outcomes.

If I think back to my educational training in the late 1960s there was very little evidence that we thought of the curriculum in the framework of being a system. We did not consider that for us to transform the classroom we needed to be aware of the requirement that our classroom must be a system comprised of inputs, a process of some kind, outputs, and an environment in which the components exist. In fact, where our transformed classroom does not have the inputs of a body of knowledge or a method of presenting the material the effort is doomed. With the body of knowledge in place, we need a process of how to instill this body of knowledge into the computer called the student's brain. With the body of knowledge in place, then we must equip the student with the ability, as Dewey said, to use that knowledge in a fashion that benefits all the stakeholders of the process.

The final component in the system thinking[8] view is that we need to have an environment in which the system operates. At this point in the growth of our students, that environment is the transformed classroom. The transformed classroom must be based on student learning to the best of his or her abilities.

Cease Dependence on Mass Teaching Methods

Return for a moment to our discussions of the legacy classroom. The legacy classroom was, and in many cases is, based on the view that the educated child will learn a standard body of knowledge based on the age and grade level of the student. This standard body of knowledge is pushed out to the students through a series of teaching methods grounded in the lesson plans and the developed curriculum. Further, the education community has developed these standard methods for delivering the information. The problem is that in many cases it does not work. We have students who, for a number of reasons, never successfully achieve the learning levels we strive to reach.

The transformed classroom recognizes that not every student learns the material in the same way. In fact, the website Learning Styles Online[9] suggests that our students learn in seven learning styles, four of which are prevalent over the remaining three, that we as humans use every day. It is also vital that depending on the situation a student may use more than one of these styles in the process of understanding the information being relayed by you, the educator/facilitator.

Some of your students will learn best when they are presented with an assortment of pictures. They learn best when they can see the issue at hand. For example, there is a story in business circles of where the management of a company was told that there was a problem with the ordering of gloves for the factory due to differing prices for the gloves. The visual learners saw the problem when they could see the varying prices labeled on each glove pair.

Some of your students will learn best when they can hear the problem described. They are the ones who learn best when you are speaking the information to them, much as you do in a lecture environment.

Still other students will learn best when they utilize words in written material such as a book, a case study, or a similar method. They are the ones who will read the documentation of a problem.

Finally, some of your students learn best when they can feel the problem. They learn when they can touch the problem and feel the effect of the situation. For example, you are presented with a piece of equipment that is not working properly, and they get the opportunity to handle that equipment and find out why it is not operating properly.

So, what is the alternative? Eliminate the tendency to remain glued to a standard way of presenting the body of knowledge. Replace the delivery of the body of knowledge through a project-based learning delivery method. We are seeing today a move to training our educators of the future to present the body of knowledge through project-based curriculum. The principles of this movement can be found in the project management and continuous process improvement efforts used in many of our business operations globally. It requires the educator in the transformed classroom to change their role from a diffuser of information to a coach/mentor/facilitator. It is through this effort that the TLS Continuum presented in Chapter 3 comes into play.[10,11]

Think back to the first time you tried to touch a hot stovetop. When we were brought into this world we learned life's experiences through experimentation. The first time you approached the stovetop and reached out, you got hurt. The next time you approached that stovetop you stopped to determine whether the reach to the stovetop was worth the pain. The transformed classroom must be the equivalent of the stovetop.

In the lower grades, the coach-mentor-facilitator educator will in most cases need to provide the students with the problem and discuss what the options are that are available to them. Consider the early learning tool where you need to put pegs into a pegboard. The students can exercise critical thinking skills as they determine on their own which blocks fit into which hole.

In the upper grades the process is no different, except the coach/mentor/facilitator sets the stage for the project by presenting the scenario of where the difficulty is and allowing the students to determine what the problem and the solution are. Many educators fail to remember that your students are instructed on how to resolve issues in their science classes by using the scientific method. Those same steps can be used in any number of subject areas. But we don't, because it is not in our area of responsibilities.

The coach/mentor/facilitator begins the process by describing a scenario. Maybe it is a particular battle. Maybe it is an election issue. Maybe it is climate change. The scenario is not the end-all of the process. With the education professional's guidance the students begin the process by determining why something is happening (the hypothesis) and then continue down the rest of the TLS Continuum steps to determine what is causing the hypothesis to take place and what are the available solutions. The project ends when the students as a group select the end solution, and the implementation steps.

The project-based learning efforts lead to a vital outcome for society and our business organizations. First, the students get experience in working on cross-functional teams and how to get along with others. Second, the project causes them to critically think about the various factors that could cause the scenario to take place.

There is a wide variety of information on the Web in the area of project-based learning and its implications for the marketplace.[12]

Drive Out Fear

Think back over your life. How many times have you been criticized because you came up with either a different solution or a different method of arriving at an answer because you did not match the "prescribed" answer?

How many times have you or a family member tried something and failed at work, only to have it appear as part of your end-of-the-year performance review?

When we respond to alternative views in this fashion, we instill in the recipients the belief that they should not "experiment" to arrive at solutions. To transform the TLS Continuum classroom, it is necessary to reward experimentation. It is self-defeating if we use project-based learning and expect the students to thoroughly explore possible solutions only to tell them if they solve it any other way than what the teacher expects that they are wrong.

The key to the transformed classroom is to provide the environment where the student feels that they are free to explore wide ranges of solutions not just a select few. They need to understand that they will not be punished by not responding in the expected fashion. The installation of fear helps no one, not the student, not the coach/mentor/facilitator, nor the society as a whole. The opposite is that the student feels free to express their suggestions or ask questions.

End the Practice of Rewarding Students Based on Numerical Testing

In my opening words about the transformed classroom, I made mention that teachers today are teaching to the test. Every time you turn around, the student is being tested for some thing or another. Here is the fallacy in this approach. Not every student tests well. Many students freeze at the sight of these tests. Instead of basing the success or failure of a student on test scores, judge students on how well they are able to master the skills of problem solving. The A on a biology exam is not a good indication of how they will function in the business world. My wife is fond of saying she took algebra in high school and probably has never used those concepts again. It is far more critical that we coach the students in problem-solving skills rather than striving to get higher standardized test scores.

Break Down Barriers between Subject Areas

One of the keys to success in the workplace is the ability to work within a cross-functional team environment. By its very nature a cross-functional team works across all ends of the organization. When we introduce project-based learning into the classroom, the students should be exposed to the same concept. Each assigned project should look at the solution from all aspects. They can improve their writing skills through the end report. They can improve their math skills by looking at the cost factors of a solution. They can look at the decision process to see how business would utilize the same skills.

Remove the Barriers to Pride of Ownership on the Outcomes

Whether we are talking about the classroom or the workplace, our ultimate goal is to have students and employees alike engaged within the organization. Students having a true stake in the outcome of their project work obtain this high level of engagement. It is critical that the students understand through the coach/mentor/facilitator that their opinions and suggestions have some value to the outcome of the project.

Our business organizations require this level of employee engagement, and it is of benefit for the view to be learned early. This is accomplished by ensuring that every interaction with the student demonstrates that the value of the student is shown. As I have already stated, the coach/mentor/facilitator does not put down a student for having the "wrong" answer or for using an alternative solution that gets to the same place as was expected. The primary goal is not the solution but how you got there.

Institute a Rigorous Program of Education and Training

The process of creating a transformed classroom does not happen in a vacuum. To be successful at the transformation it required that every person with a stake in its success from the students to the coach/mentor/facilitator to the administration be able to answer several questions.

The first question is *what is in it for me?* Everyone must understand why, here and now, the transformed school has made the decision to take this track going forward. They need to understand what was going on in the legacy school that brought about the decision to transform the school.

The second question is *how do we begin the changes?* Just telling the stakeholders that you are going to make these changes to the classroom does not explain to them how you are going to change the classroom. The steps to get there must be clearly defined and explained using the learning styles I discussed in the previous section.

The third and final question is *what does the future look like?* Everyone from the parents on down needs to clearly know what to expect in the way of student performance. Homework assignments may not be similar to what their parents had when they were in school. The method of grading student performance will inevitably look different.

Once we have educated everyone on the new normal, it is then incumbent on the coach/mentor/facilitator to train those students who fall below expectations. The coach takes the students and helps them obtain the new skills at a level where they can function in this environment. This training can be in the form of one-on-one sessions or further reading in the process.

Take Actions to Create the Transformed Classroom

Hey, I totally get it. The human tendency when trying to make change is to procrastinate. We all did it in college when we waited until the night before to begin to write that term paper. However, this transformational change does not happen overnight. This transformational change does not happen without a concerted effort to do so. It is critical for the coach/mentor/facilitator to take the change process into his or her hands and move forward deliberately to achieve the transformation. Obtain the input from all the active stakeholders as to what steps are required and follow through on those steps. Create a dynamic communication plan to let the stakeholders know how you are progressing.

TLS Continuum Transformed Classroom Case Studies

The purpose of *The Excellent Education System: Using Six Sigma to Transform Schools* was to provide you with a vision as to how, utilizing the existing school dynamics and the TLS Continuum toolbox, we could create an educational system that excels in preparing the members of the future workforce with the skills to meet the demands of that workplace. In Chapter 4, we discussed a tool called benchmarking.

Business organizations and many school districts have used it for years. You are planning changes in the school so you reach out to your fellow schools to see what they are doing in this field at present. You want to learn what works and what has not. These are all examples of benchmarking. It should be noted here that the results from benchmarking could have either a positive or negative effect on your schools.

In trying to bring our discussion regarding transforming the classroom to a natural conclusion, I wanted to find a way to demonstrate through benchmarking what others have done along the way toward implementing these tools within the classroom. At the same time, my goal is to present to you evidence-based information that would explain the process improvement path so that no matter what learning style, you would be able to draw the same conclusions that back up the classroom transformation.

The *Merriam-Webster Dictionary* defines a case study as a published report about a person, group, or situation that has been studied over time or a situation in real life that can be looked at or studied to learn about something. Those of you who have had experience studying case studies know they typically come in the form of a multiple-page document, which in narrative form presents critical information regarding the events under consideration.

The following three case studies have each used the TLS Continuum toolbox in a transformed classroom situation.

List of Case Studies

Case study 1:
   Organization: Russell County, Alabama Schools
   Situation: Jeremy Garrett's high school science and math classes
Case study 2:
   Organization: Columbus, Georgia Public Schools
   Situation: Matthew Redmond's high school science and math classes
Case study 3:
   Organization: Menomonee Falls, Wisconsin Public Schools
   Situation: District implementation of the toolbox

At the end of Chapters 8 and 9, we will use the identical format with case studies on the administration changes and how to begin the process of implementing the transformation into the schools.

TLS Continuum Transformed Classroom Case Study: Russell County, Alabama Schools

The Russell County Schools are located in southeastern Alabama along the Georgia border with a population of 55,000 residents,[13] of which 2,000 residents are students in the district's schools. More diverse than most of Alabama's school districts, the Russell County Schools are 59% African-American.

Among their high school faculty is Jeremy Garrett, who teaches math (algebra 2, precalculus, and calculus), physics, and career tech and who wrote a series of articles that were posted to the Pulse section of LinkedIn. The first of these articles was titled "How Lean Six Sigma Saved My Teaching Career."[14]

Jeremy Garrett said in his article "Prior to studying Lean Six Sigma my teaching quality could have been described as 'adequate' (which is not very complimentary). I worked long hours, hated many aspects of my job, struggled to evaluate potential new ideas, and feared parent conferences (which occurred way too often and which were nearly always negative in nature). My studies of Lean Six Sigma taught me to identify the internal and external customers, to hear the voice of the customer, to recognize the (often conflicting) needs of the various customers, and to think about my own work from a new perspective. Rather than evaluating my teaching and my curriculum and my tests from a perspective of 'correctness' or 'correspondence to state standards' (both of which are important), I learned to evaluate my work based on its 'fitness for use' by the 'customer.' Similarly I learned to treat parent communications in a new way that focused on 'ease of use' rather than 'time invested' or 'factual correctness' (even though both of these are still important). I also learned to evaluate my teaching and grading by using a mixture of qualitative and quantitative methods, including the use of control charts. I then learned to use those charts and other data to conduct a 'root cause analysis' rather than relying on intuition alone."

In particular, he utilized control charts to define week-to-week averages on classroom work. The data from these was used to detect how students responded to the work. With this data Mr. Garrett was able to show the administration what changes to lesson plans needed to be made to maximize student learning. It showed at what point the teacher needed to loop back and reteach a certain topic due to a student not grasping the concepts. The control charts also showed how best to curve the grades in class. Mr. Garrett described an example in which he discovered that he had changed the method and content of a class topic as the day progressed. The result was that the first class of the day might have received less detailed content than the last class of the day.

His ongoing application of the TLS Continuum toolbox also assisted in the grading process. He discovered that in his analysis, the needs of the students are better presented. If, on one hand, the deviation from the bell curve is small, in a non-critical situation there may be no action called for. If, on the other hand, the deviation is large, then you may need to change the approach. Mr. Garrett uses the formula of multiplying the grades by a number slightly below 1 (0.9 to 0.8) and then adding a number that both compensates for that multiplication and provides an additional shift—typically 10%–30%.

From his experience, Jeremy Garrett has been able to identify that if we use control charts, histograms, and observational data we can determine when the problem occurred and follow that with the implementation of the root cause analysis (Ishikawa Fishbone tool) and the 5 Whys, so we can determine what the exact problem is. We then can present the problem in the form of a Pareto chart to determine future direction.

In the previous case study, Jeremy Garrett has demonstrated that the tools of the TLS Continuum can have a major effect on the way the classroom instruction cycle is presented. The use of control charts and histograms tell us when what we are doing in the classroom is working, or when it is not. The use of the tools is grounded in the concentrated effort to discover how to make our classrooms better, run more efficiently, and in the long run cheaper through the students learning in a way that meets their direct needs.

TLS Continuum Transformed Classroom Case Study: Muscogee County Schools, Georgia

The Muscogee County Schools are located in southwestern Georgia along the Alabama border with a population of 200,579 residents,[15] of which 32,853 residents are students in the district's schools. Among the faculty in the high school is Matthew Redmond, who teaches science, math, and engineering. He is certified as an American Society for Quality engineer, manager of quality and, organizational effectiveness. He is also a certified Six Sigma Black Belt. His goal is to instill in his students the ability to be involved in process thinking, an understanding of cause and effect, and a high level of comfort when using data related to their process and developing a continuous improvement mindset. I asked Mr. Redmond for a brief description of how he uses the TLS Continuum within his classroom in each of the areas. This case study represents his thoughts regarding his classroom techniques and the TLS Continuum.

Process Thinking

Mr. Redmond set up instructions for tasks and projects as a sequence of steps. In this regard, he often would put these sequences into a flow diagram to demonstrate how the flow diagram could be used. The flow chart would steer the conversation toward talking about the task or project as a process. When students ask questions about a project, the flow chart allowed the discussion to be about the steps in the process rather than a list of tasks. For example, in his robotics class, students are asked to write a process flow diagram for the actions the robot is supposed to accomplish. Following the development of the flow chart, the students then use the chart to develop the computer code to run their robots. The action causes the student to break their high-level actions into a sequence of behaviors demonstrated by the robot to complete the flow chart. The end result is that the students simultaneously learn to decompose a process as well as how to program the robot.

Understanding of Cause and Effect

In those cases where a student fails to complete an assignment, Mr. Redmond uses the instances as a way to consider cause and effect. This is also used when a student has an error on a physics or math problem. The student is encouraged to determine whether the error was caused by a careless error, a lack of understanding, a calculator error, or poor penmanship or the use of the available space on the paper. The study of root cause and effect helps the students to learn that with every action there is a reaction, whether it is positive or negative.

High Level of Comfort when Using Data Related to Their Process

Prior to the beginning of each school year, his students are exposed to the concepts of central tendency and variation in their math classes. In the process they have learned about mean, median, mode, range, and standard deviation. While they have learned these concepts, they have not internalized the way the concepts and statistics relate to things they can see and feel, leading to a disconnect from experience. To counter this condition, Mr. Redmond has the students take measurements on wood cubes that they will use later for a puzzle cube project. Once the measurements have been completed they manually calculate the mean and standard deviation of the width of the cubes. The data is then imported to Excel spreadsheets. Frequently, students graduating from high school do not have the basic understanding of how to use cell formulas. They then learn to compare the computer-generated result with their hand-developed results and look for why there are any differences in their calculations.

With this data in hand, the students are shown how to create graphs of their data. The data is transformed into histograms, and they see how the visual view of the data relates to their standard deviation. This approach gives the students the experience of working with the normal distribution rather than working on data that was generated by someone else.

Development of a Continuous Improvement Mindset

Many of Mr. Redmond's students do not spend much time on the tenets of the TLS Continuum, but they do learn the design process, which is an iterative process in his robotics and automated system classes that is similar in nature to the DMADV[16] process for design for Six Sigma. As part of this process, the students learn how to brainstorm both as a concept and in real-time use. This leads to hands-on exposure to a decision matrix used to select potential courses of action. This leads to Mr. Redmond offering feedback about how the process could be done in a different way so that the students learn how skills can be built upon each other to improve the long-term process.

All these areas of concentration lend themselves to a hands-on approach to education similar to what I examined in the discussion of project-based education. Mr. Redmond has begun using the melting of aluminum in a homemade furnace fueled by charcoal. It provides the opportunity to discuss the states of matter, the composition of aluminum cans, melting points, and safety. The cans are melted in the furnace, and the students begin to discuss what they see as the cans are melted. Once the aluminum is melted, the students get experience pouring the molten material into sand molds. This provides the students with the opportunity to observe and discuss the cooling process and the behavior of liquid and solid aluminum.

In the review of the case study, we can see how the TLS Continuum toolbox can be utilized in the transformed classroom. While the first two studies are applicable to a high school-level class, the same tools in differing degrees of usage can be applied to the middle school and upper elementary students.

TLS Continuum Transformed Classroom Case Study: Menomonee Falls, Wisconsin County Schools

Either in the case of designing a training program or for the purpose of being included in a book such as the one you are holding in your hands, my criteria for selecting a particular case study can be refined to a handful of reasons.

First, is the information presented by the case study creditable? The information has to be creditable in that it is believable by the reader. Does the information align with the life experiences of the reader? Are the facts something that the reader can comprehend?

Second, does the case study present verifiable examples of strategies that can be used in your classroom or administration? Is the information able to be supported by the general public if an inquiry were made?

Third, does the case study present both actions and strategies that are repeatable and can be taken into your classroom? Without an elaborate effort, can you take these concepts and apply them in your world?

It is rare that you find a case study example that truly fits all three criteria to the fullest. The Menomonee Falls School District fully meets these three criteria. The district actually fulfills the criteria both in the transformed classroom and the transformed administration. As a result, the school district case study is presented in two parts. The first is the use of the toolbox in the transformed classroom discussed in the current chapter. The look at the toolbox use within the transformed administration will appear at the end of Chapter 8.

Menomonee Falls is a community located in the suburbs of Milwaukee with a population of 35,828 residents. The school district services a student population of 4,019 students.

What I advocated in Part 1 was that to use the TLS Continuum toolbox, you had to see the problem, feel the problem, and create the new normal. In 2007, the school district saw the problem when the *Milwaukee Magazine* ran its annual best schools report and identified the Menomonee Falls School District as one of the most underperforming school districts in the Milwaukee metro area. The district was plagued by tightening budgets and a changing education environment in the state as a whole. The result was that the school board determined that they needed to change the focus of the district. One of those changes was an endeavor to bring business improvement methodology into the school district at all levels. This change required a different view of education. It meant that instead of a staid view of the world, the schools had to look at the classroom as a business with anticipated outcomes. It required the school administration to view the classroom as a system rather than a unique entity. To further help this change along in 2011, the district hired Patricia Fagan Greco from the West Bend Joint School District #1.

Her mandate from the board was to bring this new methodology to all facets of the district from the classroom to the front office.

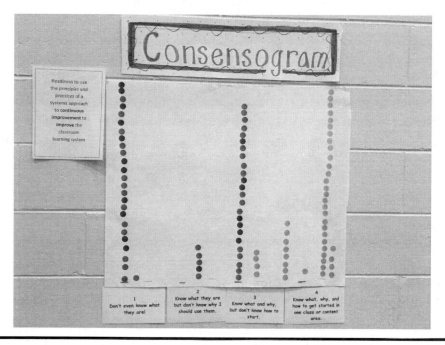

Figure 7.1   Menomonee Falls School District consensogram.

The basis of any successful continuous process improvement effort is the upfront education that is provided to the organization. It needs to explain not only what the change is but also why the change is being made. In the case of the Menomonee Falls Schools, the why is centered on the poor performance of the district. As a result, the school district creates a training program for all the members of the school district staff. This training is based on responding to a vision statement which calls for "readiness to use the principles and practices of a system approach to continuous improvement to improve the classroom learning system." Notice that the vision statement requires the staff member to look at the district from a system approach. Part of the training involves explaining to the staff member that for it to be a true system, there are certain requirements that need to be present.[17] The responses to the vision statement were recorded in a tool called a consensogram as shown in Figure 7.1. The consensogram is not an educational tool per se, but it can be used in any situation where you need to assess the level of understanding of a process.

Used at the beginning of the district's education effort it categorized the staff responses in four ways.

The first group consisted of all the staff that had no idea what the district was talking about. Most likely they had never heard of the principles and practices of continuous process improvement nor did they have any idea what a system approach to education consisted of. This group is the one most likely to feel that the way they have always done things in the district was sufficient. This group represents the staff in need of the most education and training in the new normal for the district.

The second group responded to the vision statement with the belief that they knew what the principles and practices were but it was in name only. They knew the concept behind the tools; they just did not know how to use the tools in real time. This group at least is more likely to see the problem but may not understand the effect of the problem on the transformed classroom. Their training efforts involved exposure on how to apply the tools. They see what the tools are but don't see the applicability to the education system. Like many human resource professionals they don't grasp the language of business applicability to the school. Their belief is that they are there to "teach" the students, not be business people.

The third group responded to the vision statement by indicating that they knew what the principles were and why they exist but did not know where to start the process. They see the benefit of the principles and practices but have missed how to implement the problem-solving method that is presented to them. These are the ones who need to be reminded that the process is no different than what they did as students in a science classroom.

The final statement is that they know what the principles and practices are and understand how to implement the concepts within one class or content area. These individuals see the problem, feel the problem, and understand how to bring about the new normal through change in the classroom. These are individuals like Jeremy Garrett and Matthew Redmond in our first two case studies.

It should be noted that if you change the nomenclature of the four groups, the consensogram could be used with students in the classroom to resolve the problems being studied in the project-based learning at the upper elementary grades and higher. The use of a consensogram is not limited to just four responses; in the classroom you can create as many response categories as fits the process under consideration.

Following the training, the district implemented the education into the curriculum while supplying coaches who understood the tools and how to implement them. The purpose was to coach along the instructional staff when they encountered difficulties with the new normal in the classroom.

The implementation within the classroom and with the students utilized the plan-do-study-act (PDSA) format as shown in Figure 7.2. This is similar in construct to the Six Sigma plan-do-check-act cycle. The student was asked to begin by planning the process. This established the goal for the process, when it would happen, and how the result would be measured. This created the creditable, verifiable data that was needed to prove that the goal was achieved.

Following the planning stage the class moves to the do stage in which the students indicate how they will learn. During this phase, both the student and the teacher lay out the responsibilities of each in reaching the planned activities. It also provides the milestones of the project that provide the evidence as to whether we have achieved the goals.

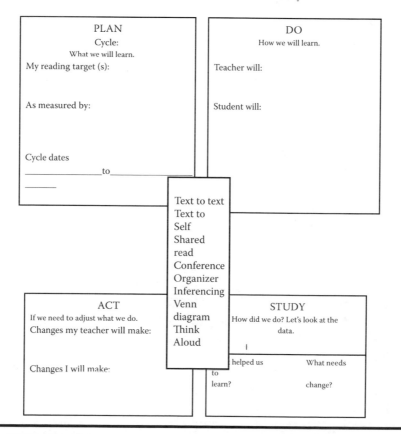

Figure 7.2   PDSA template.

The third stage of the process is the study phase. This is the point where we look at what we have done and ask ourselves what did we learn, how did we go about doing it, and what still needs to be changed.

The final stage is the act phase. With every experiment there are always things that do not go as planned, so in the study stage we look at the process and see what has to be changed and then assign the responsibilities. As in the do stage, there are separate lists of responsibilities for the student and the teacher.

The proof as to whether what I have proposed here is working is to look at the results from districts like Menomonee Falls. In 2007 they were one of the worst performing districts in the area. Jump ahead 9 years, and the district today is internationally recognized for its continuous process improvement to the point where they now present a 2-day boot camp to show others how it is done. The results on student tests show high American College Testing (ACT) scores and record participation on advanced placement (AP) tests with 80% earning passing scores. Further, the district is now partnering with higher education to align the curriculum with potential future careers.

The transformed classroom can be a reality. It entails a new focus with a view on systems rather than a one-size-fits-all approach. But changing the classroom is only one side of the picture. It is still critical that we transform the administrative side of the organization.

Notes

1. Goldratt, Eliyahu. *Necessary But Not Sufficient*. Great Barrington, MA: North River Press, 2000.
2. Taylor, Melissa. http://www.parenting.com/blogs/mom-congress/melissa-taylor/what-purpose-education.
3. Wesleyan University. http://www.purposeofschool.com/philosophical/.
4. More information can be found at http://www.bls.org.
5. More information can be found at http://www.corestandards.org/.
6. Definition of critical thinking from http://www.criticalthinking.org/pages/our-concept-and-definition-of-critical-thinking/411.
7. Senge, Peter. *Schools that Learn*. New York: Crown Business, 2012. Pp. 269–301.
8. Miller, Lawrence. http://www.lmmiller.com/wp-content/uploads/2013/06/Whole-System-Architecture.pdf.
9. More information can be found at http://www.learning-styles-online.com.
10. Suerken, Kathy. *The TOC Learning Connection*. Self-published, 2014.

11. More information can be found at http://www.bie.org/about/what_pbl.
12. Cox, James, and John G. Schleier, Jr. *Theory of Constraints Handbook.* New York: McGraw-Hill, 2010. PP. 787–810.
13. Data from the US Demographic Census.
14. The full articles can be found at http://www.linkedin.com/pulse/ how-lean-six-sigma-safed-my-teaching-career-part-1-jeremy-garrett.
15. Data from the US Demographic Census.
16. DMADV stands for Define-Measure-Analyze-Design-Verify.
17. A system is made up of inputs, a process of some kind, outputs, and the environment in which these components exist, as described on P. 552 of the *Theory of Constraints Handbook* edited by James Cox III and John Schleier, Jr.

Chapter 8

TLS Continuum and the Administration

Neither the transformed classroom nor the transformed administration can operate in a vacuum. The two operate in a symbiotic relationship with each other. The administration cannot operate without the instructional staff, and likewise the instructional staff cannot operate without the administration. They are both a vital part of the TLS Continuum transformation of the schools.

The desired outcome of the transformed school is to be the personification of our definition of educational excellence. The symbiotic relationship of the instructional staff and the administration must be grounded in the four components of the excellence definition. The transformed school must care more about your school and its stakeholders—the students. The transformed school must be willing to risk more than others think safe to change the culture of the school system. The transformed school must not be refined by the lack of insight into where the school can go once you introduce the changes suggested in this book. Finally, the transformed school must be open to the potential of what the symbiotic relationship can mean for the future of the school.

To achieve this end result, the transformed school must ensure that everything that is done in the name of transformation must be done in alignment with the goals, vision, and mission of the transformed school. This must apply not only to the district as a whole but also to the individual school. In addition, the transformed school system needs to establish a school mantra that strives to ensure that the processes within both the classroom and the front office are running efficiently. The ultimate goal is that the needs of all the stakeholders, including the students, are met. Dr. Carol Ezeugbor, in her article titled "The Administrative Process," states that the role of the administration is to integrate all the resources at hand for the improvement of teaching and learning.[1]

Legacy Administration

Like the legacy classroom, examples of the legacy administration abound in our educational systems. We have legacy administrations that are grounded in non-change. We have legacy administrations that are stuck in the kind of rut pictured by the Chick-Fil-A® commercial in which a woman states that her co-worker is in a rut because he gets the same breakfast every morning.

If the educational community is pushing for innovation in our schools, why then do we have the existence of legacy administrations? There are a myriad of reasons why the legacy administrations exist.

First is the belief that educational institutions are non profit entities. This means that every dollar that comes in from whatever source must immediately be expended so at the end of the fiscal year there is a zero balance. I totally understand this. I fully understand that the state legislatures and the federal government dictate the amount of incoming funds. The difference, as we will see later in this chapter, is how you look at the funds.

Second, the legacy administrations are stuck in a rut. They have been doing the same thing for so long that they wear a rose-colored set of glasses. Unless forced, their standard response to new ideas or processes is "that is not the way we do things around here." It is the same attitude I discussed in the previous chapter on how we do things in the classroom. They have created this standard of work based on a past work environment, and that past standard is no longer valid given today's climate for change in our educational system. They are administrations that discourage any attempts to change things for fear that they may fail in the effort.

Third, the procurement process is both cumbersome and inefficient. The legacy procurement process ties the hands of the administration due to statutes and the wrong end game. They tend to look at the wrong end target because they do not think they have any alternative.

Fourth, the legacy administration is left with a lack of a common vision. The delivery of non-standard learning outcomes from the legacy classroom is carried to the school as a whole. There are numerous examples through the school of non-value-added activities or waste within the system.

Transformed Administration

Moving from the legacy administration to the transformed administration requires that the school, as an entity, create a new normal for the school culture. It is new normal based on seeing the problems that exist, understanding how they affect the educational system as a whole, and making the necessary changes going forward. Like I did with the transformed classroom, there are clearly some changes that must occur. These changes represent the characteristics of the transformed administration and of the transformed school as a whole.

Initially, the transformed administration needs to create a constancy of purpose for the improvement of education. Unlike business organizations, the changes to the organization can only be delivered from the top down rather than a combination of both management and the teachers. From an open dialogue between administrators, teachers, and system stakeholders a new directive must be established for the school system. This new directive is centered on the idea that the primary purpose of a school system is to deliver education and learning to the students. With the end goal in sight all parties must create the purpose that everything you do or say must lead you to improving the school system every day. I recently saw a plaque in a doctor's office that stated, "Every day is the opportunity to change your life." Every day is the opportunity to change your schools. Enter your office each and every day with the intent to make those small changes in how you undertake your responsibilities, which in turn will have the greatest impact on your stakeholders and the students. David Steinberg, founder and chief executive officer (CEO) of Zeta Global, has said that innovation does not have to be about creating the light bulb or the telegraph. Innovation can be very important small changes to something that is already working. That is the stuff that is overlooked, and it can take things to the next level. Note that we are not necessarily talking about wholesale changes to the system, just ways to make it run more efficiently.

With the constancy of purpose in place, the process requires the establishment of a new philosophy on how the transformed school functions and operates. What is missing in the new philosophy is the response "that is not my job" when asked about improvements. What is missing in the new philosophy is the response "that is not how we do it around here." The new philosophy aligned with the constancy of purpose, demonstrated by all involved, is that we are open to doing whatever is necessary to improve the deliverables of the school system. The new philosophy is open to looking at new ways to do things, even if there is a chance you will fail in the attempt. You must be willing to experiment with ideas that might be contrary to the old school culture. There are some typical excuses why any organizations won't go down this road.

First is that we are talking about a school, not a manufacturing thing. The TLS Continuum is a problem-solving method, it is not a solution. Ken Miller, in his book, *We Don't Make Widgets*,[2] suggests that every process has its widget. In the case of a government agency, the widget is the permit. In the case of the school, the widget would be the quality of the education delivered to the student along with the diploma showing completion of the study of the body of knowledge. When you understand that you do have a widget, then these tools I have been discussing do have a vital role in the transformed school as you create that new philosophy.

The second excuse is that we have tried that and it did not work. The real question is, did you try using the right tools, or did the administration have the right attitude toward the effort?

- If the administration entered into the improvement effort with the belief that it would not work, then the odds are that we are confronted with a self-imposed outcome.

- If the administration entered into the improvement effort and some of the members of the administration behind your back are telling staff and teachers "don't pay any attention because it won't last," it will not succeed. Successful transformation of the schools requires that the effort be entered into with an open mind as to what the solutions are. Successful transformation of our schools requires a total commitment to the change process.

The third excuse is that it is too complex for most organizations. It may be, and then again it might not be. I do not expect all of your staff or you to be PhDs or statisticians. There are software programs on the market that require you only to enter data points, and they will complete the analysis for you.[3] The process of change is only as complicated as you as administrators make it.

With the new philosophy in place, the focus changes away from the use of mass processing and curriculum. Like I stated in the previous chapter, the concept of mass curriculum was created back in the 1600s. It since has become a mandated thing from the state level. However, the problem is that administrators get locked in the model. The administrators believe that there is only one way to do things. Administrators do not have a realization that there may be a better way. I get it. I understand that to ensure that our next generation is prepared for the workplace of the future, there are certain concepts that have to be learned. I understand that in many cases state statutes mandate this body of knowledge. I understand why this is. On the flip side of the coin, schools could learn very effectively from businesses that are successfully utilizing the ROWE[4] method of business. In that model, the successful delivery of the curriculum is the end result—how teachers get there should be left up to them. The edict is that as long as the students can show they have gained the required body of knowledge to move on in the system, how they got there is not an issue. This will require a change in the mindset of not only teachers but also administrators who are used to being so ingrained in a particular way of doing things. I can remember from my days in the classroom with principals who demanded exact lesson plans, not just what was going to be taught but how it was going to be taught. This requires the administration and state lawmakers to have an open mind to the outcomes and likewise to sign on to the new model. It will mean a period of trial and error to find what works.

To implement the new philosophy, we need to change the way we go about acquiring products and services. Many businesses and many government entities such as educational institutions have for a long time believed in the purchase based on the lowest bid or the lowest possible cost. While the appearance is that the school is working to provide the most value at the lowest possible cost, this trend comes with some inherent risks to the school. Bob Lohfeld in his 2012 commentary on the website Washington Technology[5] suggests that low price contracting leaves out of the equation any added value to the pricing. This leads to two additional factors that need to be taken into consideration.

The first factor is, does the contract price include the determination of the total ownership costs of the purchase? Are you considering all the associated costs? What if the school purchases the product or service for $1000, and the ancillary support costs an additional $1000 over its lifetime—what is the true cost to the stakeholders? Take, for example, the next computer purchase that you make for either the school or the classroom. There has for years been a heated discussion regarding the costs of Macs versus PCs. The belief is that because the PC from Microsoft is always much cheaper than a Mac, it is the better purchase. According to Jamf, when you look very carefully at the total ownership costs of Macs versus the comparable PCs, Macs win out as being less expensive in the long run.[6] Jamf points out that when you add on the extra costs that Microsoft charges for added software and support, the long-term costs are more than if you owned a Mac.

The second criterion is how do you, as a school, determine the cost of the product or service?

Like many businesses, schools determine the cost based on what many financial people are taught under the concepts of cost accounting. In cost accounting, when making a purchase the monies are allocated to each book, each pencil, each piece of audio-visual equipment, and so on. The problem is that it assumes costs before they are actually spent. As you spend the funds they become account receivables, meaning that you still have to receive the product or service. There exists in the business world an alternative to the cost accounting approach. It is called throughput accounting (TA).

TA uses primarily three performance metrics—Throughput (T), Investment (I), and Operating Expense (OE). These metrics are a simplified methodology that removes all of the mystery of accounting and rolls it into three simple measures. Instead, TA is focused on cash without the need for *allocation* to a specific product. Eliyahu Goldratt, as explained in the book *Focus and Leverage* by Bob Sproull and Bruce Nelson,[7] stated that when using throughput accounting we do not consider the purchase cost of any value until you actually spend the money (Figure 8.1).

TA is determined by taking the throughput (total costs) and subtracting your operating expenses, which results in the organizational net profit. To

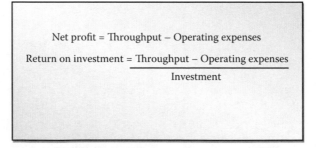

Net profit = Throughput − Operating expenses

$$\text{Return on investment} = \frac{\text{Throughput} - \text{Operating expenses}}{\text{Investment}}$$

Figure 8.1 Throughput accounting formula. (From Sproull, Bob, and Bruce Nelson, *Epiphanized,* **New York: CRC Press. PP. 248–249.[16])**

arrive at the return on investment, the result of the net profit is divided by the amount invested into the organization processes.

In the process of researching the material for this work, I was told that TA would not work in an educational setting due to its reliance on creating a net profit. Since the schools do not run a profit at the end of the year per se, it is not applicable.

What if we changed the TA model, would it then be appropriate? What if, instead of net profit, we changed the model from net profit to the through-put of the student through the system? Everything we do from the trans-formed classroom to the whole transformed school must be centered on the throughput or movement of the student through the system. Throughput in an educational environment is more concerned with the time duration to deliver your stated goals rather than for a net profit.

Ask the State of Utah government if the new model works. They have created the SUCCESS Framework[8] that applies the TLS Continuum to all of the agencies of the state government (Figure 8.2).

Under the SUCCESS Framework net profit is eliminated, and our focus is diverted from a reactionary one to one in which the transformed school pro-actively plans, schedule resources, and reduces chaos that come about by constantly fighting fires. The result is that the transformed administration experi-ences a decline in time and resources devoted to reactive responses that could be better devoted to increasing the student throughput through the school.

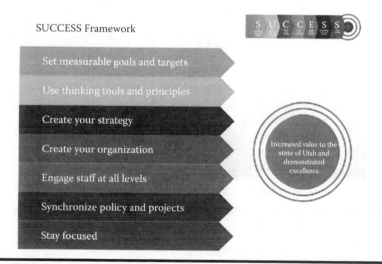

Figure 8.2 Utah's SUCCESS Framework. (From the Utah State government document "Guide to Measurement." https://gomb.utah.gov/wp-content/uploads/sites/7/2015/11/SUCCESSMeasurementGuide.pdf.)

I am by no means an expert on the SUCCESS Framework, but after conversations with Kristen Cox, executive director of the Utah Office of Management and Budget, I can clearly see how the framework can be applied to the transformed school. The framework is built around seven basic fundamentals, each of which has direct applicability to the transformed school. Following are those fundamental building blocks and how they apply to the subject matter at hand.

Fundamental Number One: Set Clear, Measureable, and Ambitious Goals

If your school were to implement the SUCCESS Framework, you would begin by setting clear, measureable, and ambitious goals. The goals selected need to have a direct relationship to increasing the student throughput in the system. So while a stakeholder may suggest a goal for the system, unless it affects the throughput the suggestions should be discarded. As we are no longer considering the net profit of the transformed school but rather a throughput goal, it is critical that the goal be clearly stated. The goals should be formatted in such a manner that everyone from the maintenance person to the superintendent of schools can understand their intent. The TLS Continuum refers to the use of stretch goals. These are goals that have been established for your transformed school that are not an easy reach but are still within the cone of reasonableness.

Once the goals have been established you need a way to measure whether those goals are enhancing the flow of students through the system. When we measure a goal, or anything for that matter, we produce data points. When I create data points I am looking for three characteristics in choosing whether to use that data. First, they need to be creditable. Creditable means that the data comes from an "experiment" of some kind that produces the data. The second characteristic is that the data points must be verifiable. If I look at your project, can I find the same data points? The final criterion for selecting a particular data point is whether it is repeatable. I want to understand that if I complete the same project under the same conditions, I will arrive at the same results.

When you have completed the first fundamental, you should have in place distinct answers to the first of three questions that will be answered at the end of the fundamental implementation. In the end the goals should assist us in putting more students through (throughput) the system more effectively and at less cost.

Fundamental Number Two: Use Data, Analysis, and Thinking Tools

The second essential part of the SUCCESS Framework is to use the thinking tools and principles of the TLS Continuum toolbox that we discussed in Chapter 4. It should be stressed here that the outcome of the tools is not suggesting a solution. The thinking tools and principles are, as I discussed earlier, a problem-solving process.

You have set your goals and you have determined how you are going to measure your progress, but before you can do that you need to find the obstacle that is holding up the system. The obstacles are those parts of the process that hold up the throughput. In the case of the transformed schools it might be the policies or the processes. It might be the resources that the administration has made available to the school system as a whole.

Once you have identified the obstacle, you want to consider how to get the most advantage out of the obstacle. Why is that obstacle present in the first place, and why did it appear? Once you have gotten the most you can out of the obstacle you want to make it the primary piece of the work in process (WIP). So, anything else going on in the school becomes secondary in importance until you remove the obstacle from the system. With those other areas diminished, the primary emphasis becomes how we remove that obstacle.

The first step in the obstacle identification is to run an Ishikawa Fishbone. The purpose is to determine how the various factors within the transformed school are affecting the goals and their achievement. With the results of the fishbone in hand you can then move to the Theory of Constraints five steps.

It is crucial to understand that you will not be successful in using the thinking tools unless you are willing to take one more step, and that is to challenge assumptions. You can't remove an obstacle if you say the effort won't work. You can't remove the obstacle if you operate from the belief that it is not the way we do things here. You can't remove the obstacle, if you believe that it is not your job to do so.

The final step is to implement the TLS Continuum. We use the TOC to identify the obstacle. Then we use Lean to remove the obstacle, and finally we use Six Sigma to create the standard of work. Finally, we ensure that there are no variations in the processes going forward.

The use of the data analysis and the thinking tools will enable you to answer the last two questions. First, how well are you doing what you do? Are you meeting the goal, and if not how far off are you? Second and finally, it will demonstrate what the current and future states of the transformed schools are costing the system.

Fundamental Number Three: Create the Strategy

With the goals in place, it is now critical to success that you create a road-map to achieve these goals. The roadmap provides the steps that need to be taken to reach the goals of the transformed school. Part of the TLS Continuum effort is to identify what needs to change; what you are going to change it to and how you are going to get there. This is the basis of school innovation strategy.

Strategy can be defined[9] as a method or plan chosen to bring about a desired future, such as the achievement of a goal or the solution to a problem or the art and science of planning and marshaling resources for their most efficient and effective use. These are the true expected outcomes from the transformed administration.

In Chapter 4, in the Define stage, I discussed at length the use of a part of the toolbox called the project charter. The charter provides a review of the proposed experiments and the steps to discover whether they resolve the obstacle(s). The charter begins with a description of the goal in the form of a problem statement. From there the charter lays out the elements of the change process and the steps that will be taken to reach the end goal.

As you create your strategy, the end result needs to be, how do we increase the throughput of the system? In other words, how do we increase the number of students that flow through the system? Part of that decision is to identify the key levers or key performance indicators, which provide the impetus for the coming change to the new normal.

Within the charter is the need to identify your team that will undertake the change process. You are identifying your stakeholders and the contributions they will make to the overall effort to transform the school. An essential part of creating your organization is that everyone within the transformed school knows the full process inside and out. Through the use of tools such as process maps, the entire organization must understand the flow of information and materials from the front door to the back door. Like the Menomonee Falls School District, everyone needs to understand the TLS Continuum methodology. They need to understand how the throughput flows through the system along with everything that influences that flow. It involves a commitment on the part of both the transformed teacher and the transformed administrators to carry through on the effort to create the new normal.

Another part of creating the organization is to strive to drive out fear of trying. As stated earlier, the creation of the new organization and the accompanying strategy is very similar in nature to the use of the scientific method in your high school science class. If we do not experiment with alternatives we will not discover the best end result. If we do not experiment with potential solutions, we do not have the ability to discover what works and what does not. If we do not experiment, we fail to fully explore the impact of the potential solutions on the organization, the new normal, and the goals alignment.

Every change you begin must be aligned with the school's goals, missions and policies. The end result of this effort is that you want to flatten the layers of the organization and determine who has the responsibilities for what functions. The goals, missions, and policies represent the target, while the change represents the arrow to get you there. If the change is not aligned with these items, it would be the same as if you shot an arrow at a tree and got the side of a house. The change would have no success at creating the new normal.

The final step in creating your organization is to establish the appropriate ratio between administrators and educational professionals. If your goal is to increase the throughput of students through the system, what is the right number of educators per student compared to the right number of administrators per teacher?

Fundamental Number Four: Create the Organization and Culture

With the roadmap in place, the next step is to create your organization. To complete this task requires that everyone within the transformed school knows the organization inside and out. Like the Menomonee Falls School District, everyone needs to understand the TLS Continuum methodology and its effects on the new normal. They need to understand how the system flows and how each action or process implemented in the district influences that flow. It involves the selection of the project team that guides the project along its processes. It involves everyone being able to create a process map so that those of you who are visual learners can understand the components of the new organization. Like creating the strategy, the development of the organization and culture must not be hindered by failing to try even though the effort may fail. As long as your organizational culture is founded on firm ground you need not be afraid to take the steps required to create this new environment. There will inevitably be some efforts to create this new organization and culture that will fail and that is a good thing as it tells us what will not work.

The important part of this effort is that we must ensure that the basis for the new organizational structure and culture are rooted in the district's goals, missions, and values. It is this trio that becomes the mirror as to whether we are on the right track going forward.

The final step in creating your organization is to ensure that everyone is on the same page as to why these developmental changes are taking place. The organization needs to communicate to the stakeholders why the new normal is creating the transformed classroom and school.

Fundamental Number Five: Engage Employees and Stakeholders

The fifth part of the framework is the engagement of the organization. It is crucial that everyone from top to bottom of your new organization be involved in the change. It means that you must provide training to everyone on why the change is necessary, why now, and what happens if we do nothing. Each party to the process must have a clear picture of the total new normal and understand that there are no excuses for not being part of the effort. It means taking your strategy that you created earlier and translating that into performance plans and actual milestones to success. The engaged administrator and educational professional alike understand what the new normal looks like and feels like. The engaged staff is able to take this information and create key performance indicators, not only for the classroom but also for the administration. These indicators have to be designed around completing the change now rather than at some later undetermined date.

Fundamental Number Six: Synchronize Projects and Policies

A key to a transformed school must be that each of the projects chosen must be aligned with the goals, missions, and objectives of the school. There are always projects that could be done, but some may not be related to these objectives. To ensure that the projects are resolving issues, you need to constantly question whether they are meeting the criteria of alignment. Every project must be able to live up to the question how does this (process, procedure, action, initiative, project, and policy) help the organization achieve its business objective? If you can't answer this in a clear way that is measureable, and where there is evidence that your answer is true, stop doing it. It is also an outcome of this synchronization effort that we reduce the level of multi tasking because of the refocus on the framework rather than trying to resolve everything at once.

The end result is a series of initiatives that result in the stakeholders having a system that allows the system to deliver a better result to the student learning environment.

Fundamental Number Seven: Stay Focused

The final part of the SUCCESS Framework is that the organization needs to stay focused on the process improvement effort. You need to work with laser focus to transform your school and the stakeholders to reach the full potential of the system through administrative meeting management, containing strategy to aligned efforts, recognition of the successes, and keeping the stakeholders in the loop.

The end result of the utilization of the SUCCESS Framework is that you are able to answer the three questions (What is it you do? How well are you doing it? And what is it costing you?) along with redesigning the throughput formula. In the new formula the quality of your system is multiplied by the number of students flowing through the system, divided by the total operating expenses to arrive at the value of the framework to your school.

In the case of the SUCCESS Framework quality refers to the effectiveness or the degree to which the school is successful in producing a desired result. Quality, on the one hand, is based on accuracy, reliability, and effectiveness. On the other hand, throughput is the demand or volume of work completed by the system or the number of people served.

This discussion of the framework is not meant to be an implementation guide but rather aims to provide you with a differing view of the value of the system. I would recommend searching for Kristen Cox or the Utah SUCCESS Framework to gain more insight into how they are doing it.

The fifth change is to commit to improving constantly and forever the system of education. Each and every day of the school year, teachers and administrators must come to work with the understanding, and the goal is to look at every process in place and ask the question, how can we do it better? Each and every day, the teachers and administrators must be willing to make the investment in experimenting with the process to determine how the schools can be transformed to bring about a system that works in the best interest of the students. Some of the changes will fail; others will take the schools to new heights of efficiencies and effectiveness. Every day the stakeholders in the system must be cognizant of what might be working and where problems are arising. Once these problems are discovered it is incumbent on the system that you take steps to remedy those problems as long as they are aligned as I discussed previously.

In line with the aforementioned strategy, it is critical that we remove the barriers to ownership of the transformation effort. This change effort is not an administrator's project. This change effort is not an educator's effort. This change is not a stakeholder's project. This change is a partnership between all three entities. This change needs to be believed from the perspective that it is everyone's project. Taking a page from the business side of the table, when employees believe they have a shared responsibility for the outcomes they are more likely to become engaged in the outcomes.

Earlier in this chapter I talked about the system needing to educate the stakeholders on why the transformed school needed to undertake this effort, why now, and what the future will look like. It is equally important that the stakeholders be encouraged, if they so choose, to take the education process further and they be given the path to do so. Menomonee Falls School District and, as you will see in Chapter 9, Gateway Technical College have laid the groundwork to do so. You should understand that once you start down this path it is a game changer for you personally outside of the system. You look at the world with a new set of lenses, and you become addicted to learning more. If I had been a typical student, I would have purchased the required books for my Back Belt (four different titles) and left it at that. My continuous process improvement library now contains nearly 100 titles. Encourage the teachers and administrators alike to go out and seek more information. Read some of the titles in the Further Reading list at the end of this book. Contact your local colleges and see what courses you can take to better understand the system. Consider earning advanced certifications in process improvement.

The sixth and final change that is required is to take action to accomplish the transformation of your schools. True transformation does not happen through osmosis. It requires active involvement in the effort. Become committed to the strategies we discussed in this chapter. Like most humans, we tend to procrastinate when we are uncomfortable. I understand that, but the transformation effort requires change. It requires change now, not 6 months or a year from now. The hope that the required changes will become easier later is a myth.

TLS Continuum in the Administration Case Study: Menomonee Falls, Wisconsin Schools

At the end of Chapter 7, I presented the first part of this case study about the Menomonee Falls School District and how they had brought the DMAIC concept/TLS Continuum into the classroom. Here in Chapter 8, I want to conclude the case study by bring both sides together and now looking at the transformed school/administration.

In the May 2007 issue of the *Milwaukee Magazine*, which in its cover story discussed the best schools in the Milwaukee metropolitan area determined by who was getting the most bang for the buck, the Menomonee Falls School District was ranked as one of four most underperforming K–12 districts. The high school was ranked as possibly needing intervention from outside the district. In 2016, the school district is now internationally recognized with regard to their continuous process improvement efforts; exceeding state expectations; students receiving record high American College Testing (ACT) scores; record participation on advanced placement tests with 80% of students receiving passing scores; creation of STEM, healthcare, and business academies; 80% of students going on to college; highest percentage of students enrolled in dual enrollment course at the local technical college. How did they achieve this turnaround?

In 2011, the district found they were in need of a new superintendent to carry the district forward. This search uncovered Dr. Patricia Greco working in a neighboring district. Utilizing the knowledge gained from her PhD dissertation on instructional practice and organizational improvement, Dr. Greco presented to the board a new perspective on education. She talked about performance metrics being used for planning purposes, not punishment. Of the metrics being a path to encourage experimentation. Of understanding the transformed school as being able to run business principles of constant improvement to improve the way we deliver our product or services to the students.

Intrigued by the picture that Dr. Greco presented, the district offered her the position and approved $400,000 to set up the program. Dr. Greco reached out to the community and local and national consultants who had been active in this area, including Jim Shipley and Associates,[10] The Studer Education Group,[11] StriveTogether,[12] and Waukesha County Technical College,[13] for assistance in the transformation.

With the consultants in place, the district selected their top 30% of employees to be trained as the train-the-trainer, giving the initial team specific training on evidence-based leadership and the basics of the DMAIC methodology. It then became their responsibility to go out into the district and train the remainder of the 300 staff members.

With the training in place and the staff understanding the expected changes, Dr. Greco went back to the board to ensure that what she was planning for changes within the district were in alignment with the board's goals, mission, and policies.

With the alignment and training regimen in place, the school district implemented the DMAIC process. It needs to be indicated that while the intent of the DMAIC process remained the same, the district modified it by asking different questions. These modified questions were more in alignment with the SUCCESS Framework described previously. As indicated earlier, the district began by questioning what was important to the district. The conclusion was that what was important was the flow of students through the school system. This was followed by asking how well was the district creating the WIP within the district? The difference between the two questions determined the system gaps. The remaining questions then moved on to determine the appropriate solutions and how the district was going to guarantee that the district would live up to the performance levels that were established.

Created by Kaplan and Norton, the balance scorecard is a visual presentation of the system operating within your workplace. It explains at a basic level the various perspectives within the organization and how they are interdependent. The responses led to the development of a Balanced Scorecard[14] for the district to track the results of the improvement effort.

The Balanced Scorecard created by the Menomonee Falls School District consists of five pillars, each with subsets as shown in Figure 8.3. Each of the pillars works through those areas that the district considered to be most critical to the achievement of the school goals. It is critical at this juncture that we look at the five pillars shown in more detail.

The first pillar begins with what we determined was most important, the flow of students through the educational system. The quality achievement

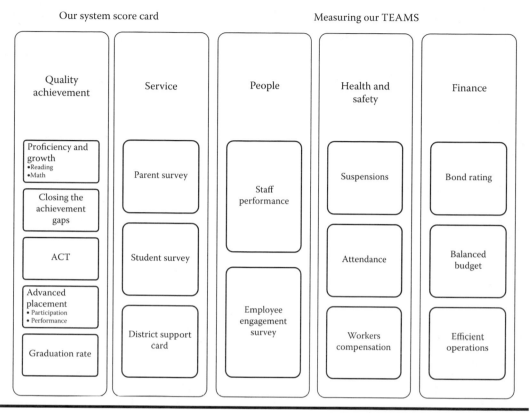

Figure 8.3 Menomonee Falls School scorecard.

pillar answers that and in turn is composed of five subsets—proficiency and growth, closing the achievement gaps, ACT, advanced placement, and the graduation rate. Each of these subsets presented a picture of where we are (how proficient are we?) and where we need to get to so as to reach the future goal.

The first subset is concerned with both the proficiency (current state) and growth (future state) of the students. In essence, the first subset answered the questions from the SUCCESS Framework as to what do we do, and how well are we doing it? To create a baseline, the district put the emphasis in the reading and math areas using the Common Core Standards as a key performance indicator. Further, much emphasis was placed on the performance of the high school seniors leading up to graduation, the African-American population, the economically disadvantaged, and the special education students.

The second subset looked at how we close the achievement gaps within our target groups. Take the example of Tiffany Fadin,[15] a kindergarten teacher within the district who asks her students every few weeks, "what specific things did we do in this unit that helped you learn? What things did not help you learn?" The goal here is to discover what is working and what needs to be tweaked to enhance the learning environment. The majority of school districts are experiencing gaps in achievements among the very groups that the Menomonee Falls District was confronted with. If we respond to this dilemma in the same fashion as we have traditionally done, the gap tends to be enhanced due to a misplaced view of how to resolve the issue. The district found that by using the system they have in place, the needs of all the students can be met more efficiently.

The third subset is ACT. ACT is one of the college entrance exams used by most high schools to judge the performance of their educational offerings. The average ACT composite score for the district, in the 2011–2012 school year, was 22.90. In the 2014–2015 school year the score had jumped to 23.47. Through greater student engagement the test scores climbed.

The fourth subset was the participation in advanced placement programs. There is a great deal of discussion in the educational world as to the value of these classes. In the district, the concern was centered on not only participation in the classes, but also how well the students were performing in those classes.

The fifth and final subset is that of the throughput level at the end of the system flow. By this I mean if we go back to the beginning of the system, how many students who enter the door in kindergarten leave the door of the high school with the diploma in hand? This represents the performance indicator, which demonstrates whether or not we have met our response to the question, what is important? I stated earlier that the answer was the flow of students through the system. The graduation rate is the metric that provides the data behind the question.

From the quality achievement pillar, the scorecard moves to a feedback pillar titled service. In this pillar, the district looked at the responses to two survey tools. The first one asked the students how they felt about the educational program. The second one asked similar questions of the parents. The results of the two surveys were then compiled as part of the district's support card. Each area (overall, likely to recommend, proud of school, safety and cleanliness) has shown marked improvement since the new system was introduced.

In any organization, the most important contributor to the success of the organization is the people who make the organization function. The third pillar is devoted to the staff of the district. The scorecard looks at employee involvement from the view of how well the staff has performed and, based on an additional survey tool, how engaged the staff members are in the process improvement effort.

A crucial need in any organization, schools especially, is the health and safety of the organization. The fourth pillar looks at the safety and health issues surrounding the schools. In a related area to student flow through the district, the district began this pillar looking at the suspension rates within the schools. Who is affected? Why are they affected? What can we do to bring down the rate of suspensions within the schools? Related to suspensions is the other side of the coin, and the district asked similar question pertaining to the overall rate of attendance. The final consideration in the health and safety area looked at the number of workers' compensation claims. How many accidents are happening because the school had not taken into consideration issues that put the health and safety of students and teachers at risk?

The final pillar dealt with the finances of the district. How good was the district's credit line? Have they created a balanced budget? How efficient are the district's operations? It is crucial that everyone on staff from the custodial staff to the superintendent becomes committed to the changes that the new normal is creating. The model used in the transformed classroom can and is carried over to the entire school. It begins with identifying what the school is trying to accomplish. The second step is how we know, when we arrive at a suspected change, that it is an improvement. Is it really transforming the school or merely disguising the change to make things look good? Then the third step is, what changes can result in that sought-after improvement?

With the scorecard in place and operating, the district needed to put in place the model for the future reviews of the district. The district chose the basic continuous process improvement model that has been in existence since the Toyota days. Everything the district did was based on four steps. The process began with the planning stage in which the district planned out the steps necessary to achieve the end goal of getting students through the system. Once the planning stage was complete the district then implemented those plans. The third stage was an analysis of the system to see if the actions taken were working. If they were not then the system returns to the planning stage, reworks the plan and tries again. If there is still a problem then you repeat the process. Note that there is no penalty phase for trying. The final stage is undertaken when the study phase tells us that we are operating in such a manner that we are achieving our goals, and so we then act on those results that are favorable to the outcomes.

Like all the included case studies, the Menomonee Falls School District shows you, the reader, the power of the new normal I am suggesting in this work. It leads to a more engaged organization at all levels. It leads to a new outlook on a system, which for too long needed that new outlook. The use of the TLS Continuum methodology creates an environment that brings out the entire potential of the organization for great outcomes.

To complete our journey toward the excellent educational system, Chapters 9 and 10 that follow will provide you with the path to not only implement the TLS Continuum in your schools, but in addition will discuss the school values that must become an integral part of the new school culture.

Notes

1. Full article can be found at http://www.academia.edu/15380530/administrative-process.
2. Miller, Ken. *We Don't Make Widgets*. Washington, DC: Governing Book, 2010.
3. While many businesses use Minitab there is a better alternative in QI Macros (http://www.qimacros.com) and Sigma XL (http://www.sigmaxl.com). Both are Excel add-ons and will do the data analysis for you.
4. First described in *Work Sucks* by Gail Ressler, ROWE refers to Results Only Work Environment.
5. See the article at https://washingtontechnology.com/lohfield-low-price-technically-acceptable.aspx.
6. See the article at http://www.jamf.com/blog/total-cost-of-ownership-mac-versus-pc-in-the-enterprise.
7. Sproull, Bob, and Bruce Nelson. *Focus and Leverage*. New York: CRC Press, 2015. Pp. 247–248.
8. Further information and resources about Utah's SUCCESS Framework can be found at https://gomb.utah.gov/wp-content/uploads/sites/7/2015/09/SUCCESS_Framework_Brochure_Digital_3.pdf.
9. *The Business Dictionary*. http://www.businessdictionary.com/definition/strategy.html.
10. Jim Shipley and Associates specializes in the design and delivery of Baldrige-based consulting and training for all levels of educational systems. http://www.jimshipley.net/.
11. Studer Education Group is a leading service provider focused on improving education and healthcare outcomes in organizations throughout the world. http://www.studereducation.com/.
12. StriveTogether is a national, nonprofit network of more than 70 community partnerships. StriveTogether works to ensure that every child succeeds from cradle to career, regardless of race, income, or zip code. StriveTogether helps communities identify and scale what works in education. We provide coaching, connections, and resources to help partnerships share data, align resources and shape policy. https://www.strivetogether.org.

13. Waukesha County Technical College is a member of the 16-campus network of the Wisconsin Technical College System. https://www.wctc.edu.
14. More information on Balanced Scorecards can be found in the works of Robert Kaplan and David Norton in their books *The Balanced Scorecard*, *Strategy Maps*, *Alignment*, *Strategy-Focused Organization*, and *Execution Premium*.
15. More information on how the district uses the evidence-based leadership and data can be found in the article "Menomonee Falls' use of data in school draws national notice." http://archieve.jsaonline.com/news/education/menomonee-falls-use-of-data-in-schools-draws-national-notice-b9951800z1-314501751.html.

Chapter 9

How Do I Implement the Same Program(s) in My School?

In the first eight chapters, my goal was to lay out for you, a reader, the potential for how to make our schools great again. How to turn our schools into transformed places of engagement on the part of students and staff alike. But this leaves us with the question, if the picture I presented has opened some interest on your behalf to try it in your school, how do you go about doing it?

How the program gets implemented has both a short and a long response. The short response is that you can be a trailblazer and begin to implement the process as a sole practitioner. While this method may have its benefits, it leaves out the involvement of the total school as well as only transforming your individual classroom. You may very well experience push-back from fellow teachers and administrators who are stuck in the old way of running an educational system. I am not trying to convince you not to try, just making you aware of the pitfalls.

The long answer explains that it is a bit more complicated than that. Therefore, Chapter 9 takes a look at the broader view and lays out a road-map for you to implement the new normal change in a way that drives you to success.

As you have seen, the implementation process is a unique journey. We know where we begin. You have an educational system that is failing to meet the needs of the students, which you have indicated are of primary importance. The end of the journey is not so clear. It will require some sacrifices on your part and a total change of outlook on education.

While the journey has no definable final destination, it does have in place a set of goals that generate two key performance indicators (KPIs). The KPI is that once you begin this journey there is no going back to the old educational environment. This is due to the fact that the educational environment within your school and system from which you left no longer exists. Continuous process improvement changes the landscape. The way your school operates has fundamentally changed. The old way no longer feels comfortable. Warning—becoming educated in this process causes you to look at the world through a new set of lenses. You are no longer content with the way we have always done things.

The second KPI is that the journey has created a new normal for your educational system. This new normal is characterized by a renewed dynamic vision for the future of your system. The turbulence I discussed earlier is replaced by full buy-in by all involved.

Any turbulence or layover at this point is caused by the urge to move quicker than the system allows. You become so engaged that if the problem is not resolved yesterday you feel like you are failing in your efforts. This turbulence is due to resolving one issue only to uncover a new problem area. The turbulence represents the lag time between the two projects. The new normal represents a closed cycle, which is continuously returning to the beginning of the process as we complete another improvement cycle.

There are ten very specific strategies for you to take in implementing the new normal. These strategies are (1) go and see; (2) focus on the process; (3) do it now; (4) gain knowledge; (5) educate and train; (6) break down silos; (7) Poka Yoke; (8) drive out fear; (9) always a better way; and (10) coach. To give you a better picture it is prudent to explore these strategies in more detail.

Strategy #1: Go and See

You worked hard to get through your education courses in college and to pass the state certification examinations. You are doing what you believe that you were destined to do—teach the future generations. I understand that. I have been there. I have done that. You are to be lauded for this achievement. But, a new environment is being introduced into the schools, the ground rules have changed, and seeing the problems facing the classroom can't been seen solely from within the confines of the four walls of the classroom or the corner office. The effects of this new game plan are seen both in the school and in the community as a whole. They are seen where the voice of the customer is most important to the transformed school. So while your classroom is something you earned, it is not the place in this new environment where the action is taking place.

Taiichi Ohno, the creator of the Toyota Production System, had a tool that he used in the process of showing managers what we mean by this new model. He asked his managers to assume they were standing in a circle on a factory floor and to observe the workplace around them to determine what was wrong with the process being observed. The reasoning behind the task was that you could not truly understand the problems unless you were there in person observing what was happening.

The same general idea is applicable in the case of the excellent educational system. If you want to be part of this transformational effort, you need to get out of your classroom and observe what others are doing. You need to seek out those schools that are actively involved in the new model. Some, like Menomonee Falls, welcome visitors to observe their model in real time. The Menomonee Falls School District conducts a 2-day Continuous Improvement Boot Camp that walks you through the entire process.

Following is the schedule for the August 7–8, 2017, boot camp.

Day 1

- Welcome and overview of evidence-based leadership
- Breakout sessions (setting goals and benchmarks)
- Building system capacity for continuous improvement
- Building in process to monitor progress

Day 2

- Overview of evaluation, always actions accountability
- Building always actions
- Communication and 45-day progress reporting
- DMAIC & PDSAs as processes to drive quality improvement
- Capitalizing on partnerships and key resources
- Next steps and opportunities

I would suggest that if you are going to go and see a program in action, be certain you get the opportunity to participate. It is far more beneficial if you get your hands dirty by getting involved as an active participant in the process. Google the idea of continuous process improvement and reach out to the options to get a clear picture of how the system performs. Be prepared to contrast your traditional school to the transformed school.

Strategy #2: Focus on the Process, not People (Avoid the Blame Game)

Look at your school. Look at it really in depth. When a report is dispatched to the stakeholders of the educational system with wrong data in it, who is held responsible? When students fail in the classroom or the school does not meet the expected standards, who is to blame? I have been embroiled in several conversations with business people who say the blame has to be with the person involved in the production of the report. However, let me present an alternate view.

If you look at the methodology presented in this book, the problem is almost never the people. I fully recognize that people can be put into positions who lack training or were ill-suited for the job in the first place, but that is a rarity in the bigger picture. The focus should be on the process.

Take a look at the works of Eliyahu Goldratt[1] and Bob Sproull. [2] They tell us that the purpose of the journey we are encountering is to identify the obstacles, remove the waste, create a standard of work, and remove variations. Within the excellent educational system, the purpose of the journey is to identify what is important and the gaps between what is important and how well we are doing in meeting the goal. From that identification, we take actions to remove the gaps and ensure that we continue to meet the goals as we progress through the system. In almost every case, they are not caused by human error but rather by steps within the process. The transformed school needs to understand that failures will happen. In the attempt to correct reworks in the processes, it is critical that we understand this fact of life and do not jump to the assumption that it automatically has to be the fault of the person running the process. In evolving your traditional school to the transformed school model, you need to be prepared to take the same route. You do not currently have a transformed school due to an insistence on doing things the way you have always done them. It does not encourage the students to become engaged in the process of education. As a rule we do not question the system in an active fashion. The change in focus to the process causes you to take a different view of your school.

Strategy #3: Do it Now

Many organizations and educational systems operate under what I call death by decision. They have a problem, so they analyze it to death, and it takes forever to arrive at a decision. In many cases, the nature of the problem has grown over time to the point at which the original decision is now inadequate to resolve the growing problem.

Once the decision is made to implement the TLS process in your educational system, you need to immediately begin the education of the educational system regarding the changes. You need to begin the process of identifying the human capital assets that you will have trained as Six Sigma Black Belts and get them ready to go. You need to begin surveying your customers regarding what their needs are. These needs are then incorporated into the standard of work. As the needs change, you have to immediately train the educational system on those changes.

Many educational systems and business organizations operate from a perspective of being reactive in nature. The key to success in the new normal we are discussing is to switch to being proactive. You want to identify the problems (goals) and determine the solutions before they become major problems that do not meet the voice of the customer.

Strategy #4: Gain Knowledge

The effort to gain knowledge in the new normal comes from two levels. The first level is knowledge of the educational system. The second level is that of gaining knowledge about the TLS Continuum.

To be successful in implementing continuous process improvement requires that you understand your system. This means that you need to understand the flow of students through the system along with the feeder processes that also guide the system. If the educational system requires a specific curriculum, what materials are necessary and how are they obtained? Once you truly understand the total system, the avenues for improvement become more readily available.

The second level of gaining knowledge is from a personal perspective. Continuous process improvement and the TLS Continuum is not a strategy that should be taken lightly. It is not something you get up in the morning and say—I am going to change the educational system and expect it to succeed. Part of your effort to gain knowledge should include reaching out to your local chapter of the American Society for Quality and/or to the local colleges and exploring the availability of classes to earn your certification in the methodology. Even if you begin with the green belt level, you will gain an added insight into how our systems function.

Strategy #5: Educate and Train

I recognize that in the scientific method and the DMAIC process the solution is found by a series of trial-and-error efforts on the part of the team members. I also contend that this change in educational culture cannot be obtained by a sink-or-swim attitude. We need to begin the process by ensuring that the entire educational system understands what is in it for them from the earliest point in the implementation process. This will come about from a vigorous range of educational programs that in the end compare the current state of the school and the future state of the school with a concentration on why the change is being made and how it will affect the rank and file of the educational system. The education must come from direct communication to all segments of the educational system, from the superintendent's office to the person in the maintenance department. The communications must be continuous and have a clear message regarding the direction the system is headed. One of the direct results of this effort will be the identification of those individuals who cannot or will not make required alterations in the way they perform their responsibilities. We fully understand that both members of management and rank and file are going to feel totally out of place in the new environment of a changed educational system. The adoption of project-based learning, for example, is going to be completely foreign to some. This new normal is not how they were trained to believe the school functioned. But, this is a different worldview than the one in which they grew up. It is not a bad thing if they feel they need to move on. On the flip side of the coin, the steps of the DMAIC process were undertaken to resolve a particular problem in your educational system. We looked at the problem and measured how the process is operating. We then analyzed the results for its creditable, verifiable data, which led us to make changes in the process and establish a standard of work going forward. The standard of work will quite likely lay out new methods for performing the process in the transformed school. You are left with two choices. The first is to undertake a management edict as discussed previously, and let the educational system continue to try to reach the goal based on how things have always been done. The other option is to design a teacher/administrator/student development program that takes the new process steps and train the educational system on how the new process looks and behaves. The training program must put the stakeholders in the position of understanding how the cultural changes and process changes in the long run should make their jobs easier.

Strategy #6: Break Down Silos (Create Teams that Reach Across the School and the Community)

As the global marketplace has evolved, everything we do affects the total organization. The same is true with the excellent education system. As a result, when we start acting from the perspective that something is not my job or that it is someone else's responsibility, then we find ourselves falling into the silo mentality. It is when we fully realize that, as John Donne said, "no man is an island," we realize that the reason we implement cross-functional teams is because what we decide to do will affect both the classroom teacher as well as the administration. Every part of the educational system is directly affected by the continuous process improvement efforts. In turn, we need to act like we understand that. Do not misunderstand me. I am not saying that the teachers and the administrators do not have a place within the educational system; they definitely do. However, the functional areas are a part of a much bigger picture, and to implement this new normal, we need to encompass the improvement suggestions from across the spectrum of ideas from the entire school community.

Strategy #7: Poka Yoke (Mistake Proof)

Allow me to step back a little bit and reconsider the improvement and control part of the DMAIC process. We discussed previously that once we defined the goal (what is important) and measured the results (how are we doing) and analyzed the creditable and verifiable data, we then turned to establishing how we removed the variations in the processes.

Once we established the standard of work for the process at hand, it put in place a system to ensure that there was less opportunity for making errors in the process. Our educational system operations can create this environment by ensuring that we use the same process every time we are presenting a concept. Is the same type of feedback used every time? Both the transformed classroom and the transformed administration can introduce steps to eliminate or drastically reduce the chance for mistakes. Through the use of such tools as Kanban, we can assure that the chances for error in the educational processes are diminished. In the Kanban environment, when you have a supply of "parts,"[3] a card is placed in an item's supply bin to alert you when you need to reorder new ones, so it never occurs that you do not have the item when needed.

Remember it was stated previously that one of our responsibilities is to get the service delivery when the customers want it, where they want it, and how they want it. It does not mean going back to the student or staff member stating that you know they needed delivery by next Tuesday, but we made some mistakes in following the orders, the service will be ready for delivery a week late. Rework is a variation from the customer's point of view. So, to achieve that goal requires us to ensure that we make as few errors as possible.

Strategy #8: Drive Out Fear (Students, Teachers, and Administrators Empowered to Express Ideas and Ask Questions)

How many of you have seen the television commercial in which the speaker is suggesting that the company consider starting a new television channel with a VJ and the response is laughter from the executives in the room, with one of them scoffing "What next? A weather channel?"? Suggestion boxes were started to get a handle on the pulse of employees or students.[4] It was an attempt to enhance employee engagement by collecting suggestions from employees on how to improve the workplace. The drawback was that the retribution for suggesting something contrary to management policy could and did result in terminations and in some cases, even death. This brings us to the problem present in many of our educational systems.

Whether it is a business or an educational system, the consensus is that although all suggestions are considered, many are shot down for a wide range of reasons. Do any of the following sound familiar?

"This is not the way we do things around here."
"We tried that; it did not work."

"Our stakeholders would not like it."

"That is not the way the Board wants it done."

The change in the educational system new normal brought about by the introduction of the TLS Continuum methodology relies on the premise that every staff member and every student's input has merit. I fully recognize that not everything will work every time and in every place. The difference here is that if we try something and it does not work, the recourse is not to tell that staff member or student, "You made your suggestion, and it didn't work." It is not to tell the staff member or student, "You are failing. You tried something that never should have been done, and it will affect your place in the educational system." We go back to the define page and review our plans to see if there is another route we can take to tackle the problem. It means taking the example of Tiffany Fadin and her kindergarten class in Menomonee Falls Schools and asking sincerely, what did you learn? What did help you? What did not help you? It means that you need to be willing to experiment with the full understanding that experimenting means some things will not work. There is nothing wrong with trying; it eliminates one more solution we know won't work.

Strategy #9: Continuous Improvement (There is Always a Better Way)

In the beginning of this work, you were asked to consider that you were taking a journey. It was a journey, but like none you have ever taken in your lifetime. This journey has a beginning but does not have a set ending. As we implement the TLS Continuum process, we uncover obstacles or road-blocks that impose non-value-added aspects to your processes that slow down the educational system. As the process continues, we remove those obstacles and establish a standard of work going forward. We have removed any variations from the process following the roadblock elimination. Think about the question asked of the students about what they learned from the lesson. What was of most help? What was the least help? By removing those responses that did not help, we have removed the obstacle. By ensuring that going forward those items do not reappear, we have established the standard of work and removed variations.

The result of the implementation of the TLS Continuum process in your educational system is that we have found a new method for uncovering the detriments to a well-oiled transformed school. We have done very well in meeting the demands of the customer based on the voice of the customer surveys we have concluded. But, the irony of the process is that once we remove one of the obstacles, another one shows up. We then need to recommit the process. The rule of thumb was described by Jeffrey Liker, in *Toyota Way to Lean Leadership: Achieving and Sustaining Excellence through Leadership Development.*[5] As described in the chapter on the Six Sigma toolbox, our ultimate goal was to create a standard of work for each of our processes. The key to discovering problems is that anything that varies from the standard of work is the problem. The result is that as we identify these variations from the standard of work, we find new obstacles that must be removed. Once we identify the new obstacle, we need to start the process over in its entirety, including new project charters. The usual time frame is approximately every 3–6 months.

Strategy #10: Coach

Not everything is going to work the way you plan—that is just human nature. It is imperative that your administration and cross-functional teams are there to help the transformed school through the valleys. The transformed administration needs to assist with the exploration of alternatives that will resolve those issues. The coaching has to be from a beneficial point of view rather than punishment. Remember that a coach does not create solutions, but assists in finding the solutions by the questions and observations he or she makes. It is not the role to be the single source of solutions, and it is not the administrator's responsibility to solve the issue by inserting personal knowledge or effort.

In this chapter, I have tried to present to you and your school the necessary requirements to undertake this transformational effort. It is creating a new world for both the classroom teacher and the administrator. It is a world of challenges and of excitement as you bring major improvements to the excellent educational system.

In Chapter 10, I hope to help you with some of this as I return to our definition of educational excellence and walk through a roadmap of how to get to your goal of the transformed school. I provide some defined strategies to get there by placing the efforts in three interdependent pillars of effort. I also want you to meet Gateway Technical College and the Clarksville-Montgomery Public Schools. In each case, the transformed educational system described has implemented the three pillars to the best of its ability but is still open to being better.

Notes

1. Eliyahu Goldratt was the creator of the Theory of Constraints and the author of series of books beginning with *The Goal*. I would especially suggest that you read *The Goal* and *Critical Chain*.
2. Sproull, Bob, and Bruce Nelson. *Epiphanized: Integrating Theory of Constraints Lean and Six Sigma*. 2nd edition. New York: CRC Press, 2015.
3. Parts can mean forms used in the office or the classroom as well as one-time-use materials in the science lab.
4. O'Brien, Michael. http://www.hreonline.com/HRE/view/story. jhtml?id=531781396. September 13, 2010.
5. Liker, Jeffrey. *Toyota Way to Lean Leadership: Achieving and Sustaining Excellence through Leadership Development*. New York: McGraw-Hill, 2011.

Chapter 10

The Road to Educational Excellence

I opened the Introduction with a discussion of the changing world we find ourselves functioning in and the fact that change is inevitable. At the same time, I suggested that the exceptional education system was faced with a critical and dire decision within your organization. On one hand, the decision could be made, and has been by some, that we will just ignore the change. My belief is that, if this is the path you chose, you are working yourself toward educational failure, and I believe your best path would be to put this book away. It doesn't apply to you. The other path was that you and your educational system wanted the transformed classroom and transformed administration to enter a new era of your involvement in the sustainability of the school. If that was the path you chose, and by still reading this book I would suggest that you have, then we needed to begin a journey.

It was a journey like no journey you had ever undertaken. It had a beginning but would never have a final destination. However, I have reached a point where it is time for me to hop off this train. It becomes your goal and your responsibility to continue the journey to reach educational excellence. My goal from the beginning was to serve as your introductory *Sensei*, your teacher and guide to show you the path that the journey would take within your school. The difference between then and now is that now you have the tools and the initial knowledge to make that journey easier. As a parting gift to you, this chapter will look at the goal of reaching a state of educational excellence and a collection of strategic initiatives that can be utilized by your school system. These initiatives are not the same as we discussed in Chapter 9. While those building blocks are necessary to implement a TLS environment within your school, they are not educational specific. The initiatives within this chapter will be very specific to the educational arena.

As education professionals we are faced with a critical dilemma. Like every other part of the school, we are being asked to justify the reason why we belong as part of the educational system. The school board has established strategic initiatives and organizational goals; however, for the most part we are left out of the conversation. We can no longer rely on being judged by what it is we do. This is due to the fact that what we do is no longer sufficient to serve the school board and the new normal initiatives. Times have changed, and for the most part we have not changed with them. We still have stakeholders coming to us with complaints that our educational system is not aligned with the community. This, to a great extent, is due to our non-participative work environment. We still have administrators who were raised on, taught, and expected to operate from the command-and-control model. We have administrators who still believe that our educational professionals are mere numbers that can be eliminated at will with no impact on the end goal.

The solution for us going forward is to work toward the establishment of a Center of Educational Excellence (COE) for the operation of the exceptional education system. Jon Strickler in his blog, Agile Elements, tells us that a COE is a "team of people that promote collaboration and using the best practices around a specific focus area to drive business results."[1] An educational COE is designed to demonstrate leadership, best practices, and support to the school system regarding the utilization of all its stakeholders within the school. In many cases the administration has the tendency to overlook these critical elements of their planning process. We can reach this factor by implementing the Six Sigma methodology we have discussed within your organization.

Excellence is not something that just happens. It comes from dedicated effort on the part of the entire school system. As we will discuss later in this chapter, it has to become part of the system DNA. It requires every person to be in total agreement with the goals and outcomes as to being right for the organization and its student assets. So, how do we define educational excellence?

I began Chapter 1 by suggesting that the Anonymous definition reportedly hanging on a wall at the US Military Academy at West Point was a start. It defined "excellence as the direct result of caring more than others think wise; risking more than others think safe; dreaming more than others think practical and expecting more than others find possible."

Educational excellence requires that educational professionals have a clear perspective of their schools and its needs. We need to understand how our stakeholders feel about the programs and services that they compensate us for delivering. We take proactive steps to anticipate their needs. As we listen to that little birdy in our ear telling us what the stakeholders, especially the students, feel is wrong with our schools, we take the risks to correct the problems based on the best available data, fully realizing that we may still be wrong. We need to play an active role in the pending cultural changes, no matter how difficult for you or the school they maybe. Through the DMAIC process we define what we feel the ultimate goals will look like, even if we can't prove it at the moment.

We have discussed along this journey that the way to acquire these aligned employees is to change the school culture in which they are involved in the creation of a new school culture based on the value of all the stakeholders in the process of design.

This final chapter is my review of the total picture that I have presented in this book. The transformed classroom and administration will continue to be a viable part of the school system once we are able to speak the language of business. I contend that the methods presented in this book and verified by the case studies found in Chapters 7 and 8 and here in this chapter are supporting documentation for the power of what I suggest. To be in a COE for education demands, even requires, that we go beyond the silo function that is so representative of many schools in the global educational environment.

Figure 10.1 is the simplest way to show the interdependence of the facets of the model I am proposing. As you can see, the basis for the COE model is centered around three areas—customer centric views, organizational alignment, and quality management. Each of these areas is built upon three sub-criteria to demonstrate mastery of the quality area. We will look at each of these areas next.

Customer Centric

The bottom of the first three tiers represents the process systems being centered on the needs of our customers. I have stressed since the outset that

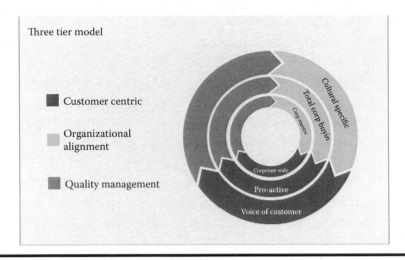

Figure 10.1   Educational excellence qualities model. QI Macros is an Excel-based software program available from KnowledgeWare. It contains the entire TLS toolbox where you just enter your data and it does the analysis for you. More information can be obtained from http://www.qimacros.com. (Part of the weekly free slide offer from http://www.slideshop.com. These slides are open source and can be edited to meet specific needs.)

the purpose of the methodology is based in a problem-solving strategy to resolve issues within the workplace. The problems have their basis in unsettling feedback from our customers that the service or product that we deliver is not meeting what they agreed to pay our organization for.

One of the best tools within the methodology toolbox is the Voice of the Customer Matrix. The Matrix is a tool that when completed fully provides a clear picture of the desires and requirements of the school system and its stakeholders. Voice of the customer is important because in this current global educational system the stakeholders are free to take their family charges wherever they want, whenever they want. To avoid this occurrence we need to find where the KPIs are not being met from the student's perspective. We talked earlier about the basis for the continuous process improvement efforts to be clearly rooted within the concepts of delivering the process cheaper, faster, and better. The Matrix is also rooted in these three concepts.

With each of the three concepts before us, the stakeholder is asked what requirements of our service are necessary for the school to meet their needs. Take getting it better, for example. On the form in the QI Macros software,[2] the suggestions for delivering a better service include (1) treat me like you want my business; (2) deliver products (or services) that meet my needs; (3) be accurate, right the first time; (4) ease of use; and (5) fix it right the first time. Each of these responses is then ranked on a scale of 1–5 based on the importance to the customer. The same process is undertaken for the remaining concepts—faster and cheaper.

From the numeric order we can identify the critical few that your educational system must react to immediately. These responses are then related to the various roles within your school system. For each stage of the process (Plan, Develop, Market, Deliver, and Support), the blocks are completed by entering the strategic actions that will be undertaken to provide the specific requirement the stakeholder is requesting.

There is, however, a disadvantage to the voice of the customer. The disadvantage is that the usage of this tool usually arises when the educational system has a stakeholder, who expresses some dissatisfaction with the school system. The educational system is thus focused on the wrong mindset.

By its very nature, voice of the customer is retroactive in nature. It is in response to a problem. The difficulty is that we are anticipating what the stakeholder wants and then reacting to the problem after the fact. Your educational system scrambles to find the quick solutions to the problems before you have a mass exodus.

Although the use of the Voice of the Customer Matrix is a critical and a necessary component of the methodology, it does not go far enough. We have to go beyond the Matrix to reach the COE status. Becoming customer centric means a more concerted effort on the part of the educational system. To become customer centric, we need to begin those cultural changes hinted at earlier.

Instead of responding to stakeholder requirements in a reactive manner, we need to change our approach to becoming proactive. The information gathered from the interaction with the parents, students, and community leaders has to place us in a position of being able to have insight into the total educational system. The organization needs to learn how to empathize with the students and learn their learning styles and challenges they face. The cross-functional teams need to take those challenges and be able to recommend solutions before they become critical problems occupying vast amounts of the time of your educational professional assets to correct problems. You want to stop becoming the school system fireman.

To fully commit to the COE model there is one more level that we have to obtain. It is important as stated that we truly hear the voice of the customer. It is equally important that we change our modus operandi to being proactive in trying to get a jump on the non-value-added issues before they reach critical points of no return. All of this effort is for naught if the change of culture does not become embedded within the educational system.

The final tier in the customer centric model is that this change must become the corporate mantra. For it to become the corporate mantra, it has to become embedded in everything the educational system does and says. The mantra is part of our educational system's brand. It is part of your mission statement. It is part of your system values. It is part of your image delivered to the marketplace. It has to be the tacit understanding that this is the way we do business because our stakeholders demand that we do it this way. If someone can't work within the new environment then they either need to get trained or leave the system. The entire process will come to a screeching halt if either the classroom or the administration decides that the old way is better and continues to be reactive instead of proactive going forward.

Customer Centric Strategic Initiative

Look at almost any school district in the country and you will find public schools and even charter schools that are underperforming compared to the data produced by the district that is provided to the state and federal government agencies. Sara Mead of the Stand Leadership Center stated in a white paper[3] that there are 843 schools in the country rated as persistently lowest achievers, 6000 schools that need to be restructured, and 1750 high schools that are rated as dropout factories. You have a school within your educational system which, in spite of the efforts to change the environment, continues to produce failing analytics on the state performance ratings. How do you determine what is needed to turn the school around? If you are like most schools, the school performance is based on the state requirements and the school planning system developed by the building principles with the approval of district administrators. This is the way it has been done for eons. The tendency is to play the blame game and state that if the school continues to underperform it must be either the presence of bad educational professionals or that the students just can't learn. Or blame the students' lack of the "smarts" to perform well on the state ratings.

Consider a different approach. Like the Menomonee Falls District, move the district from being teacher centric to student centric. I previously suggested that the goal of the school should be the number of students flowing through the system. Check with the students on how well the transformed classroom is functioning. Create the cross-functional team with the administration, classroom teachers, parents, and students to determine where the system is failing.

If asked, like in the Voice of the Customer Matrix, they will gladly tell you what is working and what is not. From there, you can design your curriculum around the characteristics that the students have said are important to them. Take the time to talk with the ultimate user of the student output and find out what their demands are and align the educational process within those desires. Understand what their expectations are and take the extra mile and meet them, better, faster, and cheaper. As Tom Peters would say, create an environment of WOW!

Organizational Alignment (Culture Specific)

The second pillar is that of organizational alignment. Like every organization, our schools, either in writing or implied, have a mission, vision, or operating statement. These cultural statements delineate their district culture. The district culture tells the world who you are and what you stand for. The combination of the district culture and the voice of the customer are the keys to your organizational alignment. This combination, however, is unique to your district. You can't go down the street to your neighboring school district and find the exact same cultural components. The corporate culture is so unique that benchmarking will be of limited value. We need to begin by establishing a clear view of just what our organizational culture is and the role it plays within your organization.

An organizational corporate culture is defined in two separate but independent views. The first view is what currently exists in the organization and second what needs to be added to the organization for its future sustainability. The final corporate cultural structures are determined by the aforementioned corporate statements as to what the organization stands for and believes in and the role it plays within the community. The cultural elements are then handed down through the educational hierarchy by top management. In the long run, the educational culture explains how the various components of the district are valued within the organization. The culture determines whether your organization becomes a school of choice in the global workplace.

To reach our Center of Educational Excellence, the entire community must be actively involved in the district cultural development discussions. The students must be involved to explain the learning environment they want. The parents must be involved to discuss what they expect from the educational institutions. The area business community must be involved to explain the skills they need from their human capital assets. The administration must be involved by setting the tone of the schools. HR is challenged with the responsibility of ensuring that the organization hires the right persons, for the right positions, at the right place, and at the right time. This means that HR must be sure that first of all the talent being brought into the educational system is the right fit for the district culture. At the same time they have to be able to determine that the new talent acquisition has the correct skills to perform the responsibilities of the position. If the skills are lacking, then a system must be put in place to develop those skills—both those developed by on-the-job training and those developed from learning a new skill, such as learning how to work with others who may not have the same acumen that your assets have toward the organization. HR also understands that nothing is forever, so the district alignment piece involves the development of a vibrant succession plan to replace those at the top utilizing the internal talent at your disposal. The change in the district culture becomes the new normal. You have the responsibility to ensure the new normal becomes the way of life within the organization. You are the ones who develop the assimilation paths.

The final tier in the culture-specific pillar is the total and complete buy-in from the organizational components to the point where it becomes the walk and the talk. The message coming out of the excellent educational system should be the same no matter who is speaking it—the superintendent or the clerk in the mailroom. Think about the parrot who is speaking—the message will sound the same. It comes from continual practice and repeatable actions.

Organizational Alignment Initiatives

As part of your organizational alignment strategies ask your stakeholders what employee development programs they need or desire. Ask them where they need further coaching about the continuous process improvement methodology. Let them tell you what would be of most value to them in aligning themselves with the new normal within the district's organization.

In that way you will not only meet the needs of the administration, but you will develop more engaged educational staff.

Quality Management (TLS Continuum)

The final, but not the least important, pillar is quality management within the model. If we change the educational culture, or believe that we have, and still make errors in delivery we have not achieved anything at all. Ford Motor Company has adopted the statement that "Quality is Job One." It has become not only their goal but also part of the corporate mantra.

What we are seeking are employees who on a consistent basis are aware of the organizational and educational processes and how they are operating. They are completely embedded in the process success and are the first ones to report when the system is breaking down. In his books, Jeffrey Liker refers to the *Andon System* in which any human capital asset has the ability to stop the process if it does not meet the established quality standards. In essence, the commitment to quality management means that when employees see a problem within a process, they not only have the authority to report it, they also have the responsibility and authority to fix the problem then and there. If the student tells you that a teaching method was not working for them, you have the authority to change the way the material is presented. If that means stopping the process until the problem is corrected then that is what happens.

As described by both Jeff Cox[4] and Bob Sproull[5,6] in their books, the process to achieve this quality management focus is the use of the TLS comprehensive review of the organization. The TLS perspective begins with using the TOC to determine the non-value-added activities within the process that are impeding a free workflow. Based in the concept of critical thinking, the TOC critically looks at your educational system with the intent to identify the bottlenecks that hold up the free flow of learning through your processes.

Frank Patrick of Focused Performance[7] provides a look at the basis of Six Sigma and TOC. For discussion's sake I will concentrate, at this point, purely on the TOC side of the equation. TOC is based in the chain of the process. Every chain of events has a weakest link somewhere in the process. TOC's goal is to identify that weak link and take steps to eliminate the weak spot. It does so through the use of logic-based tools that assist in locating the link. Look at Figure 10.2.

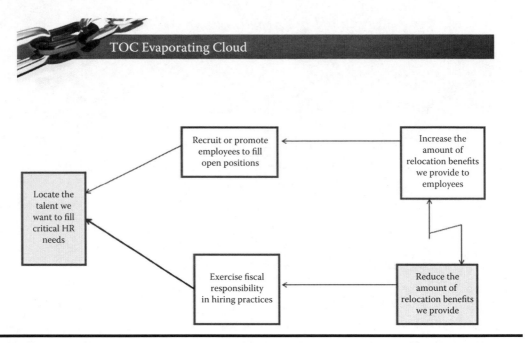

TOC Evaporating Cloud

Figure 10.2 TOC Evaporating Cloud. (From the article "Driving the Relocation 500," which I wrote for *Mobility Magazine* in 2001. http:dbainconsulting.com/ Articles?Articale9.pdf.)

One of these logic-based tools is the Evaporating Cloud. The Evaporating Cloud is designed to uncover the conflict within your processes. Consider for a moment the example in Figure 10.2. It states that one of HR's responsibilities is to locate the talent the organization needs to fill critical human capital needs of the organization. The question posed by the Evaporating Cloud is, how do we achieve that goal? The cloud offers two different alternatives. One says the goal is fiscal responsibility that requires the organization to stay within budgetary guidelines. The other option states that the goal is to recruit or promote employees to fill these critical openings.

The weakest link appears after this segment of the discussion because it directly compares the two approaches. On the fiscal side, the resulting action is to reduce the amount of relocation benefits provided to the human capital assets, while filling the positions is the paramount issue you need to increase the level of benefits. The conflict arises because you may not be able to reduce benefits and still get the level of talent that the organization is seeking. The other TOC tools then proceed to create a better picture of the weakest link resulting in a definite concept of the root cause and analysis of the problem and the viable solutions.

The bottom line is that the TOC segment of the TLS orientation provides answers to three vital questions:

1. TOC tells us what has to be changed
2. TOC tells us what we need to change the process to
3. TOC tells us how to make the change happen

The perspective then moves to the use of Lean tools to remove the obstacles and then the Six Sigma tools to create a standard of work going forward. It is this process that assists us in reaching the Center of Educational Excellence. Consider this scenario for a moment.

You have a school that is not performing to the expected levels. Using the Evaporating Cloud, you can change the components. The goal is replaced with another—provide the highest level of quality education to the students of the district. The dilemma or the cause of the problem may be that to provide the highest level of quality education we need to improve the way the material is presented compared to needing to increase the level of student participation in the planning process. The final blocks would represent what strategies must be undertaken to achieve the goal.

The roadmap to educational excellence is a journey to discovery. It is not a slam-dunk path and will never be an easy undertaking. It is about change. Change in the way we do things. Change in the very cultural aspects of your district. It is a journey designed to uncover hidden wastes that are under the radar in almost every organization globally.

I am very much cognizant of the fact that some of our educational professional peers made the decision early on to jump the train. It was, in their minds, perfectly correct to remain in the status quo. The difficulty is that they must be comfortable being the corporate fireman with the total realization that they will never reach the status of a Center of Educational Excellence. The other direct outcome is that they will continue to make the same non-value-added waste activities that they have always made because that is just the way we do things here.

Those of you who are still reading at this point are the future of the educational profession. I commend you on your understanding that in many ways the old model for education is not working. We have tried the "this is what we do," model and we still have not convinced the layers of management above us that we have a better way. Part of that frustration is because we have not done a good job at supporting our role within the educational system and showing why the new normal is more productive in the end.

This journey of discovery you are currently involved with, in this book, is a way for you to begin to make that argument.

The roadmap to educational excellence demands that you understand that you need to constantly question why you are doing what you do in the way you do. There is a tool within the methodology we have not previously discussed. It is centered around a series of questions posed to the organization. Each question begins with the word "why." The first time you ask the question you get the response that this is just the way we do it around here. By the time you get to the fifth why, in most cases there is no viable reason why a particular process is performed the way it is. You are ready for a world that is not embedded in the routine way we educate our students. The methodology that we have discussed is designed to identify, remove, and insulate the organization from activities within our processes that have no bearing on the success of our endeavors.

Our responsibility in the roadmap to a Center of Educational Excellence is that of the gatekeeper for the power of intellectual knowledge acquisition. Educational excellence is achieved when we center our efforts not on what we do but on what KPIs we bring to the table. Chief among them is the ability to identify where our student development efforts are falling short. It becomes our job to change the training effort to bring it in line with the voice of the customer.

As a professional in both the educational world and the Six Sigma world it has been a unique path for me personally, as I find that when I go to the Gemba and see what is really going on within the educational function, there is a wide array of issues that need our input to align the organization strategically. It is my hope that as we reach the end of my involvement in your journey, you continue to demonstrate the role of the transformed classroom and the transformed administration in the Center of Educational Excellence, and that you will assume the *Sensei* role, and teach the next class of professionals how to become real leaders by coaching and teaching them how to improve their segments of the organization through their unique journey of discovery. If we assume that the organization is planning on the sustainability of the organization for time immemorial, the journey is just beginning. We need to be there to guide the journey in the right direction, which will guarantee success for the future.

To a great extent, the success of your career and your organization rests in how efficiently you undertake this journey of discovery. The tools and the guidance are at your fingertips. They key is whether you take the opportunity to pursue them. Be sure not only that you educate and train the organization, but I would highly recommend that you contact your local institutions of higher education and inquire how you can get more in-depth training in the TLS Continuum/Six Sigma methodology.

The final two case studies showing how the pillars work in real time are presented next for your review. In each case they have demonstrated that when a concerted effort is applied, the new normal not only is possible but also can bring great results to the excellent education system.

TLS Continuum Implementation Case Study: Clarksville-Montgomery Schools, Tennessee

Located between Fort Campbell, Kentucky, and Nashville, the Clarksville-Montgomery Schools is the seventh largest school district in the state of Tennessee with a student population of 32,500 students in 30 schools. Trained professionals numbering 4200, from the Director of Schools office to the maintenance staff, support the student body. The easiest way to give you an insight into what has happened in the Clarksville-Montgomery Schools is to align the efforts of the district to our three pillars.

Pillar 1: Voice of the Customer

I have stressed since the very beginning of this book that the key to a successful improvement effort is to get a handle on what the customers (stakeholders) want and expect from the excellent educational system. The district achieves this goal through the use of surveys and focus groups. Surveys are conducted on an annual basis with parents and staff in areas that are deemed to be high need or that have not been conducted recently. The results of these surveys are then used to make the changes to processes. One result of the surveys was in the area of preschool registration, where standardizing the process saved the district $10,500 per year.

The other vehicle is the use of a series of focus groups to determine how the customer is feeling about the school district. Each of these focus groups is comprised of a specific population that is affected by the district processes.

On a monthly basis, members of the transformed administration within the district meet with representatives of the parents, school instructional staff, and high school students. On a bi-annual basis, the administration meets with special education student parents, the ethnic diversity parents, the military families, and the English as a second language parents. The purpose of these focus groups is to identify, through open dialogue, what is working and what is not within the district. It is from this input that the district can make the changes to answer the voice of the customer.

Pillar 2: District Specific

The Clarksville-Montgomery County School system has adopted the mission statement that the reason they are in business is "to educate and empower our students to reach their potential." Within the community, the district provides the avenues to make the necessary improvements as problems arise. Through comprehensive training provided to all the central office staff, the concepts behind continuous process improvement are responded to annually. It is a critical part of their compliance training offered at the beginning of each school year.

Pillar 3: TLS Continuum

The Clarksville-Montgomery County Schools determined that they wanted to become more effective in their delivery of the mission statement, so a previous director of schools made the decision to take the district through the process of qualifying as being ISO 9000:2008 certified. Developed by the International Organization for Standardization, the ISO standards lay a model for determining the effectiveness of your organization. In particular, the ISO 9000:2008 standards talk about the establishment of a quality management system.

Let's review those standard clauses for a moment. Clause 4.0 deals with the implementation of a quality system with the understanding that you must continually improve that system. Clause 5.0 discusses the idea of management responsibility and the demonstration of management commitment to the improvement process. Clarksville-Montgomery County Schools has established an entire system to implement the standards.

Visit http://www.cmcss.net/departments/director/departmentforms.aspx and you can find copies of the entire form list including a copy of their detailed Continuous Improvement Quality Manual.

Clause 6.0 deals with resource management, specifically the training resources. It begins with Clause 6.2.2 (a) covering the question of whether the district has the necessary competence for personnel performing work affecting conformity to product requirements. The district has in place policies and procedures to make the staff able to identify things that are out of conformity. The process in place also contains feedback loops involved in sending problem areas back to the administration. In Clause 6.2.2 (b) the district lays out the training available or other methods to achieve the necessary competencies. The district has put in place an annual training regimen given every fall to all the district staff. Clause 6.2.2 (c) requires that the district has in place a method to evaluate the effectiveness of the actions taken. This is then carried forward to Clause 6.2.2 (d), under which the district, as a matter of policy, ensures that the results of the various surveys and the results of process improvement efforts are publicly posted on the district's website for the public to see and consume.

Finally, in compliance with Clause 6.2.2 (e) the district maintains a record of all the training delivered and the skills available through the district.

With these efforts in place, I want to return to an earlier point in this chapter. When a problem is uncovered, the final committee utilized by the district comes into play. The Senior Leadership Team decides who will be the champion for the continuous improvement project. The champion will always be a Senior Leadership Team member, but the team will include stakeholders most impacted by the change. From there the champion and the administration assemble a team of subject matter experts from within the district or the community, and this group works to resolve the issues. Timing can be several months or several years.

TLS Continuum Implementation Case Study: Gateway Technical College

According to the college's website, Gateway Technical College laid the cornerstone of career training when Racine Continuation School began classes November 3, 1911, as the first compulsory, publicly funded school in Wisconsin—and, in doing so, also became the first in America.

From a single building in Racine, Wisconsin, technical education as we know it today has grown to be one of the most powerful forces in building our economy and a trained workforce.

From its inception, Gateway has provided students with education and training to pave the way for their careers and futures. Training has been tailored to the needs of the industry of the day—addressing traditional as well as emerging, in-demand career fields. Gateway continues to serve its communities by supplying local industry with trained workers and residents with opportunities to gain solid paying careers.

In 2006, with the assistance of The Quality Group, Gateway Technical College began offering training for the Lean Six Sigma methodology to local business organizations. Seven years later the college decided it was time that they walk the walk as well as talk the talk of quality improvement. The intention at the time was to improve efficiencies and reduce wastes in their operations. The goal or the problem was how to deliver a superior experience to all stakeholders. With this in mind, in the fall of 2013, the college established the Office of Quality Systems. In September 2013, the college promoted Kamaljit K. Jackson to the position of quality manager.

By April 2014, all 604 employees, including the Board of Trustees, of the college had completed the basic Six Sigma White Belt training. In the interim the college now has on staff 625 White Belts, 35 Green Belts, and 12 Black Belts.

With the establishment of the Quality Systems Office and the hiring of Kamaljit Jackson, the college established the process that any ideas for improvement of the college processes must flow through her office. While they still need to be evaluated by the college's internal advisory committee and presented to the executive leadership team, any employee is not only able but encouraged to submit project ideas to improve the college. To date, 40 projects have been submitted for evaluation. Once a project is approved, a dashboard is created for each project and managed by the director of quality systems and progress reported quarterly to the leadership team, and annually the savings are reported to the Board of Trustees. Of these 40 projects, the list of active projects is limited to six to eight at any one time. At the same time, the approved projects are awarded both the time and the resources to carry out the project to its completion. Another critical factor in this process is the selection of the right team. The leadership team develops the project teams based on the members' knowledge of the process, their experiences with the issue, and the individual strengths of the members using the strengths-based criteria developed by the Gallup organization. In fact, the entire college is run on a strengths-based approach to operations.

To date, Gateway Technical College has witnessed between 1 million and 2 million dollars in savings from the projects that have been completed, and these savings are reinvested into the programs to fund them going forward.

I talked about the idea that one part of the three pillars was a corporate mantra. Gateway Technical College reports that there was no pushback from the college employees regarding the program. Many of the teams have gone on to operate independently of the total operation by incorporating the methodology into morning huddles, Kaizans, dashboards, and so on. The three campuses are now into site-based management, and the college as a whole has developed Gateway Access that continues to communicate a standardized quality message to the college stakeholders. These are all demonstrated behaviors indicating that the college has achieved the corporate mantra as everyone has become immersed in the continuous process improvement effort.

Notes

1. Agile Elements. Center of Excellence definition. http://agileelements.wordpress.com/2008/10/29/what-is-a-center-of-excellence/, October 29, 2008.
2. QI Macros is an Excel-based software program available from KnowledgeWare. It contains the entire TLS toolbox where you just enter your data and it does the analysis for you. More information can be obtained from http://www.qimacros.com.
3. Mead, Sara. *Turning Around Low Performing Schools*. http://standleadership-center.org/what-we-stand-turnarounds.
4. Cox, Jeff, Dee Jacob, and Susan Bergland. *Velocity*. New York: Free Press, 2010.
5. Sproull, Bob, and Bruce Nelson. *The Ultimate Improvement Cycle*. New York: CRC Press, 2009.
6. Sproull, Bob, and Bruce Nelson. *Epiphanized*. Great Barrington, MA: North River Press, 2012.
7. Patrick, Frank. Focused Performance TLS Comparison. http://focusedperformance/artiles/tocsigma.html.

Appendix I: Studer Education Matrix

Studer Pillar	District Plan Goals	Goal	Core Measures of Improvement	Studer EBL Assessment Tools
Quality	Student Achievement	• District will be a high-performing school district with an enriched and relevant PK-12 curriculum that promotes creativity, critical thinking, and achievement while exceeding state and federal standards.	• Standardized tests	
		• District will have an exceptional completion rate and will graduate students prepared to enter the workforce or college of their choice.	• Graduation rates	
		• District will provide the appropriate environment for exceptional achievement for all students.	• Mean score	• Student Engagement Survey*
		• District will offer all students a wide range of school-sponsored activities outside of the classroom.	• Number of activities	
		• District will ensure that all students have an abundant opportunity to form a strong foundation in ethics and character development	• Character assessment	
Service	Community	• District will engage the community stakeholders with an active and collaborative partnership to augment educational excellence, workforce development, and quality neighborhoods. Parents, teachers, students, and community members will be active partners in the district's education of students.	• Mean score • Target score	• Parent satisfaction survey* • Service support card**
Finance	Operations	• District will use strategic plans to be fiscally responsible and efficiently use all resources – human, time, and monetary – to support student achievement.	• Efficiency ratio	
People	Resources	• District, as the employer of choice, will recruit and retain the best people by rewarding excellence and providing opportunities for continual professional growth	• Mean score	• Employee Engagement Survey*
Safety	Environment	• District will have a pervasive culture of safety and respect. AISD will have and maintain world class facilities that provide the strongest foundation for students to be leaders in a global economy	• Parent satisfaction score on safety items • Reduction of incidents	• Parent Satisfaction Survey

* Studer Education Surveys aligned to leader. *Must Haves*® to improve leader performance. Other tools are acceptable if aligned to defined categories for improvement.

**EBL contract required measurement tool developed and administered by Studer Education.

Appendix II: ISO 9000 Certified K–12 Schools in the United States

Boston Public Schools	Boston, MA
Brandywine Public Schools	Wilmington, DE
Clark County Schools	Las Vegas, NV
Clarksville-Montgomery County Schools	Clarksville, TN
Jeffco Public Schools	Golden, CO
School District of Lancaster	Lancaster, PA
Liberty Center Local Schools	Liberty Center, OH
Racine Unified School District	Racine, WI
St Louis County School District	St Louis, MO

Appendix III: Baldrige Education Framework Award Winner

Sponsored by the National Institute of Standards and Technology within the US Department of Commerce, the purpose of the Baldrige framework is to help your organization improve and achieve excellence. The questions in the Education Criteria help you explore how you are accomplishing your organization's mission and key objectives in seven critical areas: Leadership; Strategy; Customers; Measurement, Analysis, and Knowledge Management; Workforce; Operations; and Results. The Baldrige framework is based on core values and concepts that represent beliefs and behaviors found in high-performing organizations. More information on the educational framework can be found at https://www.nist.gov/baldrige/about-baldrige-excellence-framework-education.

Years	*School District*	*Website*
2015	Charter School of San Diego	http://charterschool-sandiego.net
2013	Pewaukee School District	http://pewaukeeschools.schoolfusion.us/
2010	Montgomery County Schools	http://www.montgomeryschoolsmd.org/
2008	Iredell-Statesville Schools	http://iss.schoolwires.com/
2005	Jenks Public Schools	http://www.jenksps.org/
	Richland College	https://www.richlandcollege.edu
2004	Kenneth W. Monfort College of Business	http://mcb.unco.edu/
2003	Community Consolidated School District 15	http://www.ccsd15.net
2001	Chugach School District	www.chugachschools.com
	Pearl River School District	www.pearlriver.k12.ny.us
	University of Wisconsin-Stout	http://www.uwstout.edu/

Appendix IV: Lean Tools and Six Sigma in Education

In the course of my research for this book, I had the opportunity to talk with Thomas Frederick, Lean Six Sigma Black Belt, who produced a document to argue the case for the Theory of Constraints–Lean–Six Sigma (TLS) Continuum within the educational setting. At the time, he was a member of the faculty at Saline High School and has since moved to Michigan Medicine. Following is that document.

How can a process improvement technique and its set of tools, originally developed for manufacturing, be of any value in an educational environment? It becomes clearer if you understand what Lean is, and at its core, what an educational system is. LEAN is simply an operational set of knowledge-based tools that allows for the identification and elimination of waste in any process or combination of processes to improve the efficiency and add value. Lean requires a culture change in how everyone thinks on a daily basis, and is a long-term journey of continuous improvement. Since a single school or entire school system is simply an organization made up of various processes also designed to add value, the adaptation is relatively easy. The American education system is struggling today with loss of funding, loss of enrollment leading to more loss of funding, teachers that are overextended and expected to do even more with less: the reduction of a huge number of teachers and administrators, transportation cuts to rising costs, and on and on (Lean Concepts, Inc.)

Current Hurdles to Excellence in Education

1. Learning is disorganized/fractured
2. There is WASTE
   a. Unnecessary repetition
   b. Re-teaching
   c. Unclear explanations
   d. Unanalyzed test data
   e. A systems change with every new teacher
3. There is not always a common vision
4. There is not always common outcomes (too much variance)
   a. Mr. Smith's chemistry class is not the same experience as Mrs. Washington's
   b. Ann Arbor Skyline's 9th grade English does not have the same outcomes as that of Taylor High School
5. Education is delivered as a top-down monopoly
   a. Education is teacher centric, not student centric
6. Quality improvement plans are shortsighted
   a. They lose momentum without management support over the long haul
   b. "This too shall pass...."
7. Teaching to the test instead of teaching for valid, effective learning

How Lean tools and Six Sigma changes education

- Weekly huddles between department staff or teacher with the same courses to ensure alignment of outcomes, pacing, sharing best practices
- Hearing the "VOC" shifts the focus from "delivering content" to "active listening"
  - Pull systems instead of push systems
  - We must identify all internal and external customers and meet their specifications
- Analyzing formative assessment data instead of just reporting summative data will drive instructional changes and show true student growth
- Hoshin planning/managing by policy for culture change
- Improved work instructions
  - New teachers don't have to reinvent the wheel
  - Students don't have to guess at what they are supposed to do

■ Gemba walks (learning walks) by the administration and board to get to know what is happening on the front lines and hear feedback about current problems and proposed solutions
  – Link management to those in the trenches
  – Foster sharing best practices
■ A team continuous quality improvement approach
  – Maximizes strengths and diminishes weaknesses
  – Builds trust between teachers and managers
  – Improves morale
  – Students are engaged in forming learning
  – Increases student morale
■ Helps teachers to understand their actions as a moldable, changeable process and that can be formed scientifically
■ Increased effective communications means
  – Students gain confidence
  – Less rework, more time for active learning
  – Fewer parent–teacher conferences
■ Teachers will learn to evaluate assessment data and use it to form future instruction
  – Builds teacher confidence
    • Students and their parents often seek out weakness and uncertainty and take advantage of those people and those situations, simply being confident automatically causes certain problems to never arise!
  – Evaluate teaching and grading by using a mixture of qualitative and quantitative methods, including the use of control charts.
  – Use control charts and other data to conduct a "root cause analysis" rather than relying on intuition alone.
  – Data-based, systematic, "needs driven" decisions lead to an increase in self-confidence.
  – When a situation does arise, the best way to end a parent conference quickly and positively is to show up prepared, certain, and able to justify actions, decisions, and grading methods with a sense of pride and confidence.
■ Fosters teacher innovation
  – Daily improvement idea.
  – "To work, changes must be not only adopted locally, but also locally adapted." Berwick asserts that for this to happen requires reinvention. "Reinvention is a form of learning, and, in its own way, it is an

act of both creativity and courage. Leaders who want to foster innovation…should showcase and celebrate individuals who take ideas from elsewhere and adapt them to make them their own" (Berwick, 2003, P. 1974).

■ Education/curriculum that is "customer driven"
 – A critical quality tree progression shows how you take what is important to the client (student, parent, future teachers, state board of education, universities) and translates that into what your business must do to meet those needs.

■ Reducing waste in supply or teaching materials orders

Further Reading

Cox, James, and John G. Schleier

Theory of Constraints Handbook. New York: McGraw-Hill, 2010. Chapter 26 is totally devoted to education.

Duncan, Sally, and Barbara Cleary

Thinking Tools for Kids: An Activity Book for Classroom Learning. Milwaukee, WI: American Society of Quality, 2008.

Liker, Jeffrey

The Toyota Way: 14 Management Principles from the World's Greatest Manufacturer. New York: McGraw-Hill, 2003.Liker, Jeffrey, and David Meier
The Toyota Way Fieldbook. New York: McGraw-Hill, 2005.
Toyota Talent: Developing Your People the Toyota Way. New York: McGraw-Hill, 2007.Liker, Jeffrey, and Michael Hoseus
Toyota Culture: The Heart and Soul of the Toyota Way. New York: McGraw-Hill, 2008.Liker, Jeffrey, and Gary Convis
The Toyota Way to Lean Leadership: Achieving and Sustaining Excellence through Leadership Development. New York: McGraw-Hill, 2011.Liker, Jeffrey, and James K. Franz
The Toyota Way to Continuous Improvement: Linking Strategy and Operational Excellence to Achieve Superior Performance. New York: McGraw-Hill, 2011.

Senge, Peter

Schools that Learn: A Fifth Discipline Fieldbook for Educators, Parents, and Everyone Who Cares about Education. New York: Crown Business, 2012.

Suerken, Kathy

The TOC Learning Connection. Niceville, FL: TOC for Education, 2014.

Sproull, Bob

The Ultimate Improvement Cycle: Maximizing Profits through the Integration of Lean, Six Sigma and the Theory of Constraints. New York: CRC Press, 2009.Sproull, Bob, and Bruce Nelson
Epiphanized: Integrating Lean and Six Sigma. Great Barrington, MA: North River Press, 2012.

Bibliography

Introduction

National Center on Education and the Economy. *Tough Choices or Tough Times*. San Francisco, CA: Jossey-Bass, 2007.

Center for Budget and Policy Priorities. http://www.cbpp.org/research/state-budget-and-tax/most-states-have-cut-school-funding-and-some-continue-cutting. January 2016.

Chapter One: What Do We Mean by Educational Excellence?

Liker, Jeffrey. *Toyota Culture: The Heart and Soul of the Toyota Way*. New York: McGraw-Hill, 2008.

Liker, Jeffrey. *Toyota Talent: Developing Your People the Toyota Way*. New York: McGraw-Hill, 2007.

Spear, Jeffrey. "Defining Excellence." http://www.studiospear.com/downloads/DefiningExcellence.pdf.

Chapter Two: Where Did Six Sigma Come From?

Pande, Peter, Robert P. Neuman, and Roland R. Cavanagh. *The Six Sigma Way*. New York: McGraw-Hill, 2000.

"Quality Circles." http://enotes.com/quality-circles-reference/quality-circles.

Liker, Jeffrey. *Toyota Culture: The Heart and Soul of the Toyota Way*. New York: McGraw-Hill, 2007.

Lencioni, Patrick. *Silos, Politics and Turf Wars*. San Francisco, CA: Jossey-Bass, 2006.

Goldratt, Eliyahu. *The Goal*. Croton-on-the-Hudson,. NY: North River Press, 1984.

Ulrich, David. *GE Workout*. New York: McGraw-Hill, 2002.

Chapter 3: What Is Six Sigma?

Arthur, Jay. *Free, Perfect and Now*. Denver, CO: KnowledgeWare, 2012.
Mikel, Harry, and Richard Schroeder. *Six Sigma: The Breakthrough Management Strategy Revolutionizing the World's Top Corporations*. New York: Crown Publishing, 2005.
Miller, Ken. *We Don't Make Widgets*. Washington, DC: Governing Books, 2010.

Chapter 4: Six Sigma Toolbox

Miller, Ken. *We Don't Make Widgets*. Washington, DC: Governing Books, 2010.
Arthur, Jay. *Free, Perfect and Now*. Denver, CO: KnowledgeWare, 2012.
Mikel, Harry, and Richard Schroeder. *Six Sigma: The Breakthrough Management Strategy Revolutionizing the World's Top Corporations*. New York: Crown Publishing, 2005.

Chapter 5: In Plain Sight: Sources of Wastes

Arthur, Jay. *Free, Perfect and Now*. Denver, CO: KnowledgeWare, 2012.

Chapter 6: Transforming the Educational System

Cox, James, and John Schleier, Jr. *Theory of Constraints Handbook*. New York: McGraw-Hill, 2010.
Productivity Press. *Lean Speak*. New York: Productivity Press, 2002.
Dettmer, H. William. *The Logical Thinking Process*. Milwaukee, WI: ASQ Quality Press, 2007.

Chapter 7: TLS Continuum and the Classroom

Senge, Peter. *Schools that Learn*. New York: Crown Business, 2012.
Miller, Lawrence. http://www.lmmiller.com/wp-content/uploads/2013/06/Whole-System-Architecture.pdf.
Suerken, Kathy. *The TOC Learning Connection*. Self-published, 2014.
Cox, James, and John G. Schleier, Jr. *Theory of Constraints Handbook*. New York: McGraw-Hill, 2010.

Chapter 8: TLS Continuum and the Administration

Miller, Ken. *We Don't Make Widgets*. Washington, DC: Governing Books, 2010.

Sproull, Bob, and Bruce Nelson. *Focus and Leverage*. New York: CRC Press, 2015.

Sproull, Bob, and Bruce Nelson. *Epiphanized: Integrating Theory of Constraints, Lean and Six Sigma*. 2nd edition. New York: CRC Press, 2015.

Kaplan, Robert, and David P. Norton. *The Balanced Scorecard*. Boston, MA: Harvard Business Press, 1996.

Kaplan, Robert, and David P. Norton. *The Strategy-Focused Organization*. Boston, MA: Harvard Business Press, 2001.

Kaplan, Robert and David P. Norton. *Strategy Maps*. Boston, MA: Harvard Business Press, 2004.

Kaplan, Robert and David P. Norton. *Alignment*. Boston, MA: Harvard Business Press, 2006.

Kaplan, Robert and David P. Norton. *The Executive Premium*. Boston, MA: Harvard Business Press, 2008.

Chapter 9: How Do I Implement the Same Program(s) in My School?

Sproull, Bob, and Bruce Nelson. *Epiphanized: Integrating Theory of Constraints, Lean and Six Sigma*. 2nd edition. New York: CRC Press, 2015.

Liker, Jeffrey. *Toyota Way to Lean Leadership: Achieving and Sustaining Excellence through Leadership Development*. New York: McGraw-Hill, 2011.

Index